THE
ROCKAWAY
CHRONICLES

Memories Of A Seaside Haven

JACKIE BALESTRA

KP PUBLISHING COMPANY

ISBN: 978-1-960001-63-4 (Paperback)
ISBN: 978-1-960001-64-1 (eBook)

Library of Congress Control Number: 2024924734

Editor: Laurel J. Davis
Cover Design: Juan Roberts, Creative Lunacy
Literary Director: Sandra Slayton James

All photo credits not identified belong to Rosemary Farish

Published by:

KP Publishing Company
Publisher of Fiction, Nonfiction & Children's Books
Las Vegas, NV 89117
www.kp-pub.com

Printed in the United States of America

For Mom and Dad . . . thank you for *everything*.

Map showing Rockaway Peninsula location

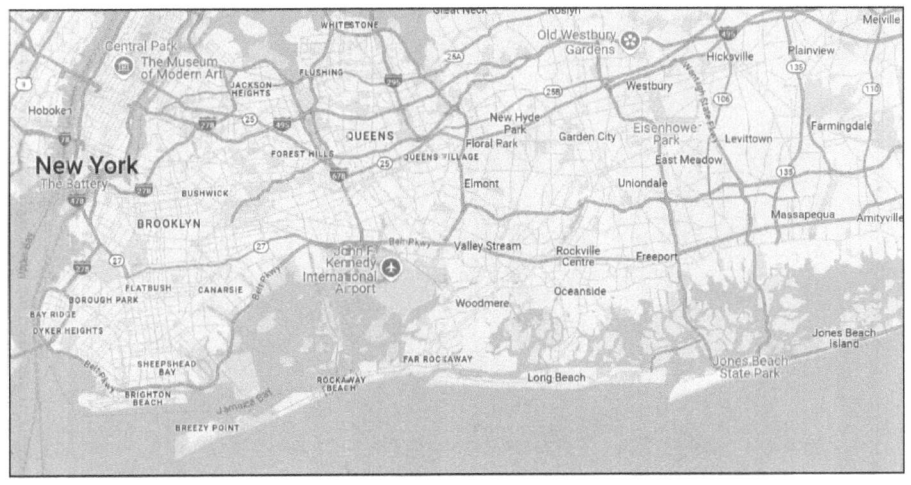

CONTENTS

Contents

Bungalow Families:
The Hollyhurst Court Years
1954–1975

Bungalow 235A:
  The Bradys
  British couple

Bungalow 235B:
  The Duffys

Bungalow 235C:
  The McVeighs
  The Negengasses

Bungalow 235D:
  The McGills
  The Gintys
  The Fays

Bungalow 233A:
  The Walkers
  Elderly couple w/dog

Bungalow 233B:
  Hellen & Buddy Nolan
  The Coogans
  Couple w/ young daughter
  Lifeguards, Glen & Steve

Bungalow 233C:
  The Farishes

Bungalow 233D:
  The Kitsens
  The Harts

Timeline

101st Street	Hollyhurst Court	1954–1975
99th Street	Upper block	1977–1980
99th Street	Frumpkin's Court	1981–1987
100th Street	Small Court	1988–1990
Breezy Point	Private home rentals	1991–1993
103rd Street	Apartment	1994–2014

PREFACE

Historically, the Rockaway peninsula supported a seasonal, coastal community. For three months each year, it was frequented by working- and middle-class families escaping the oppressive heat that descends every summer on the urban jungle known as New York City. The following is a chronicle of my childhood summers in Rockaway Beach, the salty, sandy, sundrenched landscape of my youth.

My family rented one bungalow or another in Rockaway for over forty years, but our history there goes back further. My parents had been going to Rockaway since they were kids, and believe me when I say, that was a LONG TIME AGO. They rented a bungalow in Hollyhurst Court in 1954, the year my older sister was born, and we resided there every summer until 1975.

Over the next twenty years, we rented an assortment of bungalows in various courts until they disappeared from the seaboard, and then we made our way out to Breezy Point, where we rented private homes for a few summers. My father's death played a big part in my mother's eventual decision to buy an apartment at the beach. So you see, we've been there for a while.

As a child, I assumed everybody had a summer home somewhere. When we departed for the beach each year in mid-June, I assumed that all of our city friends did the same. It wasn't until years later that I discovered this wasn't the case and realized just how fortunate we were. My family was by no means wealthy. My parents were frugal, no-nonsense, working-class folks with a healthy respect for the dollar. Even after they retired, they both went back to work part-time. I swear, the Greatest Generation possessed a work ethic that puts every following generation to shame.

While visiting my mother many years ago, I asked how we were able to be on vacation for three consecutive months every summer. She explained that my father had six weeks of vacation each year and she had five weeks, and they stretched them by commuting into the city for work. Furthermore, my mother didn't return to work full-time until my younger sister Christine and I were both in elementary school, and by that time, my sister Barbara was old enough to watch us. In all those years, it never occurred to me that it was just us kids who really had the whole summer off, nor did I comprehend the sacrifices my parents made to provide that refuge year after year.

As we know all too clearly, change is constant and nothing—*nothing*—is immune to it. Rockaway Beach was no exception. Over the course of a few decades, that quaint seaside haven slid into a steep decline. Several factors were responsible for this failure: bad urban planning and policies, alcohol- and drug-related crime, the influence of casinos and gaming, the wrath of Mother Nature, and, eventually, the apathy that can wreak havoc on a community inundated with socio-economic problems.

My family was just one of thousands that struggled in vain to withstand the abrupt changes happening around us, trying to preserve a way of life. It was a rare and wonderful time and place, which, for all intents and purposes, no longer exists.

A few of the following stories are not my own. They've become part of our family and friends' collective consciousness. It's a form of osmosis, I suppose. A story is told and retold so frequently that, oftentimes, one can no longer discern whether a particular memory is real or imposed. The first story, "The Packard," is a good example of this. I *know* I wasn't there. I *know* I never laid eyes on that particular automobile. I *know* this because that specific incident occurred a year before I was born. Still, I can see the events of that morning quite clearly in my mind's eye. My parents recounted this story so many times over the years, and with such attention to detail, that I might as well have been present. The rest of the stories are as close to the truth as I remember, along with generously provided insight from friends and family members.

Some of the names in these stories have been changed, and for others, I've only used a first name to protect their privacy.

THE '59 PACKARD

Dad a.k.a. Ibby

My father purchased a used 1959 Packard in the spring of 1961. Painted glossy black, it was in pristine condition and to say he adored it would be an understatement. He spent a great deal of time fussing over it, tinkering with it, and polishing every inch of it. He'd acquired it only a few weeks before he transported our family to Rockaway in it that summer and took every opportunity to show it off to his friends and neighbors. He made sure it was always parked right in front of our court on 101st Street where he could keep an eye on it. And while admiration was encouraged, every kid on the block knew better than to touch it, much less lean against it or, God forbid, sit on the hood.

Saturdays were always a big night in Rockaway. My parents' friends from the city frequently came out to the beach on the weekends to escape the heat. While many of them stayed at our place, quite a few rented their own bungalows in Rockaway during the summer months. Barney and Sis Geneese had a place on 45th Street in Far Rockaway; my uncle, Mickey, and his wife Georgina, rented a bungalow over on the Jamaica Bay side. Mary and Joe Lawler and Mike and Ronnie Gordon shared a huge house on 88th Street.

Early in the season, probably Memorial Day weekend, Barney and Sis Geneese planned on having a barbeque at their place and invited the whole gang. Dominick and Emily Daniello, Pat Vitale, and a few others came in from the city for the festivities. They met at our bungalow and decided to all drive to Barney's together. Dad wasn't about to let pass an opportunity to show off his car and insisted on driving everyone. So, they all piled into the Packard, showing much appreciation for the new vehicle. And off they went, my father beaming.

They arrived back at the bungalow after a fun-filled evening and to my father's horror, there wasn't a parking space to be found on our street. Parking was always a nightmare on weekends, and in the excitement of driving his friends in the new car, he'd forgotten to take the necessary parking precautions. (We'll get to that later.) As much as he hated having the car out of sight, he didn't have much choice that night. He ended up parking the car around the corner on 102nd Street.

Dominick, Emily, and Pat slept at our bungalow that night, not being in any shape to drive back to the city. Mom was the first one up the next morning and, anticipating the hangovers, decided to treat her houseguests to Italian Icees with aspirin, a Rockaway ritual. She walked around the corner to 102nd Street to buy the crushed ice treats and, having made her purchase, just happened to glance down the street where she saw a cluster of police cars with their lights flashing. Whatever had happened, it was big. So, she made a detour to see what was going on.

As she approached the scene, she saw that a telephone pole had been knocked down in what looked like a multi-car collision. And right in the middle of it was Dad's Packard, crushed by the pole and wrapped in telephone wires! Two cars in front of it and two cars behind it were all crunched together, front-end to back-end, like an accordion. Mom stood there gaping, Icees and hangovers quickly forgotten. Eventually, she came to her senses and rushed back to the bungalow, wondering how on earth to break the news to my father.

During her absence, the rest of the household had risen. My mother, never one for subtlety, walked into the bungalow, put down the cups of rapidly melting Icees, and calmly said to Dad, "Ibby, here are the Icees. Whatever you do, don't go around the block." He took one look at her face and went racing out of the house.

Within minutes, the whole gang had stumbled around the corner, bleary-eyed and in various stages of undress, and stood aghast at the accident scene. Quietly, my mother asked my father if he had run into the telephone pole the night before. He assured her he hadn't. Surely, he would have remembered hitting a telephone pole. None of his passengers recalled hitting a telephone pole, either. My parents identified their car for the police and were told that a drunk driver, who was in custody, had caused the whole thing, knocking down the pole and plowing repeatedly into the parked cars. Fortunately, nobody was hurt, for which everyone breathed a collective sigh of relief. Unfortunately, the Packard was a total loss and Dad, well . . . Dad was inconsolable for the rest of the summer.

Welcome to Rockaway.

2
THE ROCKAWAYS

Steeplechase Boardwalk, Seaside, Rockaway Beach, NY

Rockaway Beach. Long before the world became oh-so-politically correct, it was dubbed "Irish Town," a label that stuck through the 1970s. It was also called "Seaside," and on some of the old maps it's referred to as "Tent Town," but its official designation is Rockaway Beach. Rockaway Beach, New York.

Rockaway is located in Queens County on a nine-mile-long peninsula that juts out from the southernmost tip of Queens and the west end of Nassau County. On the north side, the peninsula protects islands of somewhat dry land, connected by bridges, in the swamp known as Jamaica Bay. On the other side is the Atlantic Ocean.

On the Queens approach to Rockaway, you drive along Cross Bay Boulevard through the towns of Woodhaven, Howard Beach, and

Broad Channel. Broad Channel is just that: a strip of swampland with Jamaica Bay closing in fast on all sides. Most of the structures are built on pilings. Decades ago, a large area of this marshland was designated the Jamaica Bay Wildlife Refuge. Driving through it at night, it's not unusual to catch sight of a vast array of wildlife, birds in particular. It's only a forty-minute drive from mid-town Manhattan but a world apart in every other respect.

Prior to the invasion of Dutch and English settlers in the late 1600s, the Canarsie Indians inhabited this region. They called it Rechouwacky, which means "the place of our people". Due to their inaccessibility, the beaches of the Rockaway peninsula were playgrounds of the wealthy with private yachts. By the late 1800s, steamer ferries and a rail connection provided access to thousands of pleasure-seekers from Manhattan, Brooklyn, Queens, and the Bronx. Hotels, bungalows, and bathhouses sprang up and residential communities were developed. In due course, Rockaway Beach became an everyman's paradise.

The entire peninsula is known as "The Rockaways," but it consists of several distinct communities. The landlocked end is called Five Towns and is comprised of the quietly affluent, bedroom communities of Lawrence, Woodmere, Hewlett, Inwood, and Cedarhurst. Heading west from Five Towns on Rockaway Beach Boulevard is the town of Far Rockaway, home to the only hospital on the peninsula, the aptly named Peninsula Hospital, a place where we all spent some time over the years.

Rockaway Beach is situated in the center of the peninsula, and during the late 1800s, this stretch of coastline became a summer enclave for the hordes of working-class, Irish families that lived in the city the other nine months of the year. The people who lived there referred to it as Seaside when they wanted to distinguish where on the peninsula they resided.

At its most narrow point, Rockaway Beach is only five blocks from Jamaica Bay to the Atlantic Ocean. According to maps, Rockaway Beach stretches from about 90th Street to 101st Street and Rockaway Park extends from 102nd Street to 119th Street.

Rockaway's Playland, built in 1901, was the jewel in the crown. Carloads, trainloads, and busloads of families would spend the day at the beach and the evening at Playland. As amusement parks go today, it wouldn't be a blip on the radar screen. It was never world-famous like its big sisters, Coney Island or Palisades Park. But to the folks who spent the summer in Rockaway, and the masses of inner-city families that would drive out for the day or weekend, it was nirvana.

Further out on the peninsula, just past Rockaway Park, are the residential communities of Belle Harbor and Neponsit, charming neighborhoods with large, shingled, old-style beach cottages. Belle Harbor and Neponsit consist for the most part of year-round residents. The homes actually have lawns and gardens, which is quite an accomplishment, considering the entire peninsula is essentially a giant sandbox.

Just beyond Belle Harbor lies a considerable land tract that is part of the Gateway National Recreation Area, which includes Jacob Riis Park and Fort Tilden. Riis Park has a great stretch of beach and a public golf course. Fort Tilden used to be just that—a naval base. It was one of the original Naval Air Stations and was operational from 1917 through 1930. The U.S. Navy built more than eighty structures on that site, but in 1974, it was one of several former military bases transferred from the Department of Defense to the National Park Service. Due to the buildings' deteriorating condition, most have been demolished. There are a few hiking trails out there, along with soccer and baseball fields for children's leagues. It is home to Engine Company #329 and a theater company that puts on shows and concerts.

Located at the very tip of the peninsula is the town of Breezy Point, which is easily accessible from Brooklyn by way of the Marine Parkway Bridge. Breezy is a gated, co-op community and during the last few decades has become quite affluent. At one time, Rockaway was called the "Irish Riviera"—a reference to the hard-working, heavy-drinking, fighting-mad Irish population that invaded its shores each summer. Breezy Point has become the real thing.

At Breezy Point, the peninsula is gradually growing wider and longer as ocean tides carry sand eastward. At one time, the homes built there were fairly close to the shoreline. Now, wooden walkways carry pedestrians out to the water's edge. The last time I was there, it was still quite a hike once you left the path to get to the shoreline. Due to the ever-expanding beachfront, most residents keep a red Radio Flyer wagon with their address painted on the side to convey their beach gear out to the shore. On any given day, you'll see dozens of these transports scattered about the end of the walkways, emptied of their goods, waiting to be put back into service for the trip home. The image they convey never fails to bring a smile. The beaches are truly immense, and once you are there, you find yourself surrounded by grassy dunes that are home, sanctuary, and nesting habitat to thousands of pipers and terns. If the numerous posted signs don't convince you of that, the protective, aggressive, dive-bombing birds will.

3

WE ARE FAMILY

The Farish Family: Barbara, Jackie, Dad, Mom & Chrissy

Our family nucleus numbered five: Dad, Mom, Barbara, me, and Christine. When people saw us, you could practically hear them mumble, "Three daughters, God help them." Yeah, they had their hands full with us, alright.

Barbara was born in 1954 and is eight years older than I am (1962), and I'm eighteen months older than Chrissy (1963). Dad was 50 when I was born and, by any measure, that was rather late in life to start a family. I don't think my parents really gave any thought to this momentous undertaking, much less spent time worrying about it. I mean, they were too busy putting food on the table, keeping us in clothes that fit, and maintaining some semblance of control. No doubt about it, we were a handful. But we were a happy family—loud, rambunctious, and full of character, to put it mildly. There were tough times, of course, but by and large, my childhood was wonderful. And the best of times were always in Rockaway.

Nineteen sixty-two was the year of my birth. Born in May, I was comfortably ensconced at the beach house the following month. We traditionally opened the bungalow on Memorial Day weekend each year and 1962 was no exception. My family had been renting this particular bungalow in Hollyhurst Court for the previous eight summers, so being there was no great hurdle, even with a newborn. We lived in Manhattan the other nine months of the year, and the city being the hot and sticky place it was during the summer, my parents never thought twice about making the sacrifices necessary to come up with the rental cost each year. The owner of the court, Mr. Murphy, would call my father each March and ask if we were taking the bungalow again that season. Dad always said yes. The phone call was strictly a formality since the bungalow was packed with our possessions. It was a given we would be in residence by the time school was out.

4

BUNGALOW HOPPING

Visiting the Grahman Family in Oyster Bay. In order from right;
Dad is in front looking over his shoulder, on his right is
Ronnie Gorden, Pat Vitale, Emily Daniello, Dominic Daniello,
Lena McDonald, Billy Grahman, Pop Grahman, Mrs. Grahman,
Peggy McShea, Pat McDonald, Mike Gorden.

While my parents took day trips to the beaches in Rockaway as children, as adults, prior to renting their first bungalow in Rockaway, Mom and Dad usually went to the beaches in Port Washington, the Jersey Shore, or Oyster Bay, where they had friends and family they would stay with.

When my sister Barbara was born, my parents decided it was time to get a place of their own for the summer. Mom had no desire to stay in the sweltering city with an infant. This was in the early 1950s and air conditioning was not common in households until well into the 1960s.

My parents had enjoyed their previous summer stomping grounds, but since Dad would be working most of the summer, he wanted to find a place from which he could easily commute into the city. He didn't want to drive to work every day on the Long Island Expressway or the New Jersey Turnpike, and anyone familiar with those roadways certainly understands why! The other commuting options were NJ Transit or the Long Island Railroad, but those involved multiple transfers and would take hours.

We lived in Manhattan and Dad worked in the Bronx. He took the IRT Lexington Avenue Line #6 train to work every day. The subway station was two blocks from our apartment and that train provided a direct route to his workplace. When he learned that the IND Eighth Avenue Line A train ran from the Bronx directly to Rockaway, my parents, already familiar with Rockaway, decided to look for a place there.

They found a bungalow for rent in Hollyhurst Court on 101st Street in Rockaway Park. The bungalow was at the very end of the court and they only spent one summer there. Apparently, kids from the court behind them used to throw stuff over the fence into our side alley where the shower was, and it annoyed Dad to no end. The following year, a bungalow two doors down became available and they decided to move into it. That bungalow backed up to exceptionally noisy neighbors in Cynthia Court. So, the next summer they moved into yet another bungalow. Third time's a charm, and my family lived there for the next eighteen years.

5

BUNGALOW SUBCULTURE

Dad, Uncle Tom McCloskey, Aunt Jo Farish, Mom & Emily Daniello

The Rockaways' most extraordinary physical feature, aside from the beach, was the rows and rows and rows of beach bungalows. The bungalows were developed as courts. Some courts were small, with as few as half a dozen bungalows; others were extensive, with as many as one hundred. The color schemes were universal: either white or yellow with dark green trim. Each had a porch, and I'd guess about ninety percent had outdoor showers. There were numerous single-family homes and several apartment buildings in the Rockaways, but the bungalow courts with their inherent bonhomie provided the architectural vernacular, inadvertently bestowing upon the town its unique charm.

Each court had a name and when someone asked where you lived, that's what you referred to. Our bungalow on 101st Street was in

Hollyhurst Court. On one side of us was Cynthia Court, on the other side was Berstein's, and up the block was Callahan's. Across Rockaway Beach Boulevard were Arby's and Koss. Marcel's was over on the bay side, and even though I was only six or seven years old when it was torn down to make way for the Bay Towers apartment buildings, I distinctly remember it. Auer's was on 95th and 96th Streets. All the summer people knew the name of the courts and where they were located.

Every court had its own distinct personality and social traditions, and each one had an "end-of-summer" party during the long Labor Day weekend. Some parties were small affairs with the requisite food, drink, and decorations. Others, like Marcel's, were huge blowouts complete with a band, a costume parade, and a dance contest. Our court parties fell somewhere in between. They were never the bashes for which Marcel's was famous, but we always had a huge turnout.

Memorial Day was the traditional weekend to open the courts for the summer. Most of the families went home after the holiday so the kids could finish the last week or two of school, but Memorial Day weekend was the unofficial start of summer and celebration was the order of the day. The Fourth of July was another occasion for merriment, and we were always trying to outdo ourselves. Back in the day, fireworks were legal, and we always had a massive assortment of brilliant, raucous pyrotechnics. Parties were a way of life, and the various courts and their residents were in constant, albeit friendly, competition in that regard.

In Hollyhurst Court, the women prepared the food and each household chipped in for the booze. Huge blocks of ice were bought, and the kids were given ice picks to chop them down to size. Everybody would get in the spirit when it was time to decorate the courtyard, and the inhabitants of neighboring courts would watch with interest to see what we were up to. Hollyhurst had a reputation to uphold when it came to social gatherings! The men would spend days on ladders trimming the courtyard with flags, bunting, and colored-paper lanterns. My dad provided plywood panels and sawhorses for the bar and buffet tables. Someone was put in charge of music; a phonograph would be set up and everyone would bring out their records. Parties were a full court effort and all we needed was an excuse for one. Throughout the summer, we would hit upon various pretexts for parties. There were birthdays and anniversaries, Flag Day, Father's Day, the summer solstice, and the occasional saints' days. In Hollyhurst, any reason for a party was a good reason.

Hollyhurst was a typical, if small, bungalow courtyard. There were eight bungalows, four on each side, with the front porches facing each other across a center walkway. Most bungalows were tiny since you were really only in them to sleep. I can't imagine ours was more than five hundred square feet. They were freestanding, with small alleys in between to accommodate the outdoor shower stalls. I'll never forget those showers as long as I live, simply because there's nothing quite like an outdoor shower. Some had roofs; ours didn't. We showered under the sun, in the rain and morning chill, and by the light of the moon.

The alleys in between the bungalows also were used for storage. Bicycles, beach chairs, clotheslines, trashcans, toys, pails and shovels, surfboards, inner tubes, rafts, beach umbrellas, fishing poles, shopping carts, coolers, barbeques, and the occasional go-cart could all be found there. Some people even managed to squeeze in a garden, invariably decorated with the giant, bleached seashells that washed up on our shores. The delicate conch shells you could put to your ear and hear the ocean.

The bungalows were built strictly for summer use, hence the outdoor showers. There was no insulation or drywall, so the entire structural support system was exposed, including the rafters of the pitched roof. The wainscoting partition walls were a uniform eight feet tall, which meant they only met the roofline at the perimeter of the building. Translation: no privacy. Not only could you hear everything going on in your own bungalow, but since there was no air conditioning, and the windows and doors were always open, and your neighbors were only ten feet away with their windows and doors open, you could hear everything going on in your neighbors' bungalows, as well. Courts held no secrets.

Everyone knew when a teenager came home late—God help her. We all knew when somebody was on the phone, taking a shower, cooking dinner, eating dinner, cleaning up after dinner. We could tell you what the dinner conversation was about. We could hear every argument. We knew when guests were visiting. We knew exactly when the cocktail hour started because we could hear ice being forced out of the metal ice cube trays. And everybody, including people in the next court, knew when Christine and I were getting the crap beat out of us and why.

The bungalows in Hollyhurst were identical. There were two bedrooms, a kitchen, a tiny bathroom, and the main room, which served as a living room, dining room, and spare bedroom. The only fixture in the bathroom was a toilet, so the kitchen sink saw a lot of action. We washed hands and faces, brushed teeth, bathed babies, and scrubbed dishes in it. We shucked oysters and laundered clothes in it. We shaved our legs in it and my father his face in it, and sometimes the razors got mixed up and my father would bleed in it. Being the center of activity as it was, God forbid anybody left clothes or dishes to SOAK in it.

The front porch served numerous purposes, as well. When Chrissy and I were toddlers, my father wrapped chicken wire around the railings, installed a gate, and declared the porch our new play pen. When it rained, some of the items that were usually stored in the alley came up on the porch for cover. When we had friends over for slumber parties, we would tack up sheets and put down the itchy, wool army blankets my godfather, Pat Vitale, would bring us from the Brooklyn Armory to create tents to sleep in. Friends who came down for the day often ended up spending the night sleeping on a chaise lounge on the porch. On nights when it was just too hot to be indoors, my parents would set the TV up outside and the neighbors would pull up chairs in the walkway, on our porch, or on their own and watch whatever channel the antenna would bring us. For the most part, though, the porch simply was a place to sit on rocking chairs, whiling away the afternoon listening to music or a ballgame, or chatting with neighbors. Every bungalow had rocking chairs on its porch, and I wondered for years if that's how this place got its name, Rockaway . . .

6

IBBY

Dad

My dad's name was Sylvester, but everyone called him Ibby, except for his coworkers. They called him Eddie. Don't ask me why. My friends called him Mr. Farish because when I grew up, we referred to all the adults as "Mr. This" or "Mrs. That." We were brought up to respect our elders, with a little fear thrown in for good measure.

Dad was strictly old school and from a family that was fairly well off, but that didn't mean he could slack off. He left school after eighth grade and went to work, and he didn't stop working until the day he died. When he was forced to retire from the lumberyard after forty years, he went out and found another job. For him, there was nothing more rewarding than getting paid for a full day's work. He didn't believe in handouts and would have been horrified to collect unemployment. He would have died before going on welfare. He believed in good old-fashioned, backbreaking work. If you wanted something, you worked for it. Period. Don't expect favoritism. Don't wait for assistance. And don't count on luck. His childhood consisted of two World Wars with the Depression sandwiched in between, for Christ's sake. What else would you expect? It goes without saying that we were not brought up with any sense of entitlement.

Dad was a quiet guy, generally. He worked all day, came home, read the paper, and ate supper with us every night. He was a meat and potatoes guy. I mean, he really ate meat and potatoes every night, except Fridays, of course—we being faithful, observant Catholics. If there were no meat or potatoes on the plate, then it wasn't supper and he'd look at my mother as if she'd lost her mind. He was conservative by nature and traditional with regard to social mores. There was a correct way to do things and you didn't mess with it. He was a staunch supporter and loyal member of the Republican Party.

On the other hand, when the occasion arose, and it arose quite frequently in Rockaway, Dad could be the life of the party. He was the driving force behind the many parties and celebrations held in Hollyhurst during our time there. He was the first to crack open a can of Schaffer beer for a toast, and when the opportunity presented itself, the first to get up and dance or sing a song. He worked hard, he played hard.

While my parents discussed all decisions concerning our upbringing, Dad usually deferred to Mom when it came to us girls. He never punished us. Mom meted out punishment—generously, I might add. Dad never cursed in front of us, either. When one of us pushed all the right buttons, he would puff up, clench his teeth, and call the offending daughter, "You, you, you *louse!*" That's it.

The only time I recall seeing him really angry was when Barbara's first husband, Harry, left her for another woman. Even though Barbara and Harry ended up friends after the divorce, my father would never speak to him again. When my father was on his deathbed, Harry sat in the lobby of the hospital every day, begging my mother to let him see Dad. Dad never forgave him for hurting Barbara the way he did and never gave him a chance to apologize. Nobody cried more than Harry at Dad's funeral.

My sisters and I had distinctly different relationships with my father. Barbara was Daddy's little girl and she reveled in that role. She still does. She had him all to herself for her first eight years and all I ever heard about during that time was what a little princess she was.

I was the tomboy in the family and Dad did all the things with me that he would have done with a boy child. He came to my basketball and softball games. He'd play stickball and catch with me and taught me how to throw a football. When I grew older and had some discretionary income of my own, I'd take him to Yankees and Mets games and treat him to as many hot dogs, peanuts, and beers as he wanted. On Sunday mornings, we'd sit in companionable silence watching old John Wayne movies.

Christine was the rebel in our family and her relationship with my father was a constant tug of war. She accuses my parents for not "being there for her," but the reality is that it was Chrissy who wasn't "there." She was always off doing something she shouldn't have been. She would beg to differ, I'm sure. But she's not the one relating this story, so HAH! I find it amazing that we all grew up in the same house with the same parents and had such diverse childhood experiences with my father.

My mother is a different story altogether.

7
NEIGHBORS

The Brady Family: Barbara Jean, Frank,
Margie & Mickey

While I have only a few distinct memories of my first summers in Rockaway, along with several photographic-induced ones, I clearly remember our neighbors. The Brady's were in the street front bungalow, the Duffy's in the second, next were the Negangasses', with the Fays at the end. On our side, the Walkers were first, across from the Brady's; the Coogan's were across from the Duffy's; then my family; and the

Kitsen's in the back bungalow. These families had been spending their summers in those bungalows for years.

Christine and I were the youngest kids in our court. My sister Barbara is eight years older than I, and most of the other court kids were near her age. She and Eileen Kitsen were good friends and she dated Mattie Coogan for a summer or two or three. Barbara Brady was a bit young for her to hang around with, but Mickey Brady was old enough to run with her crowd. Mr. and Mrs. Duffy had a son named Jackie who was older and didn't stay at the bungalow often, but they also had a nephew named Kenny Eslinger who came to stay with them every summer. I could never keep track of how many Walker kids there were—at the time, I couldn't count that high. Suffice it to say that Chrissy and I were a bit spoiled and tended to run wild.

Jack and Helen Duffy were always so nice to all the kids, even at our most rambunctious. Mr. Duffy was very active in New York City politics and one year was the Grand Marshall of the St. Patrick's Day Parade. That's a pretty big deal in New York City. Every year my parents took us to that parade and it was because of Mr. Duffy that we had passes for those coveted seats in the reviewing stands on Fifth Avenue.

Mr. Duffy had a regular Friday night poker game in Hollyhurst. The table and chairs would be set up in the middle of the court, but if the weather wasn't cooperating, they'd move the game into his bungalow. Mr. Duffy, my dad, Mr. Brady, and Mr. Kitsen were the regulars. Sometimes, Mr. Coogan would sit in. Often, my mother's brother Tom, known to all as "Gooch," would come to Rockaway on Friday afternoon, play cards Friday night with the guys, and get up early to play golf with my parents on Saturday morning. Sometimes, one or two of us kids were drafted to serve beer and sandwiches. We did it gladly—the tips enhanced our allowance. That's where I learned the fine art of poker and a few choice phrases that would make my mother blush. This was real poker: five-card, seven-card, the smell of cigars and scotch, the art of the bluff, and a place where the term "wild card" was never, ever spoken.

Matt and Julie Coogan had four children; their daughter, Juelanne, was the oldest; then Germaine; then came the boys, Mattie and Jackie. Barbara and Mattie were a hot item for a few summers.

Frank and Margie Brady had four children: Margie, Francis, Mickey, and Barbara Jean. Mr. Brady was a fun-loving fellow and was always up for a good practical joke. Between Mr. Brady and my father, mischief was always afoot.

Our years in Hollyhurst Court were a fun-filled period. All of the families got along incredibly well and there were many, many good times. Frank Brady, in particular, was entertaining. He always had something up his sleeve and would get everyone in the court involved on some level.

During the summer of 1964, my sister Barbara, who was ten years old at the time, decided she wanted to plant some flowers in front of our bungalow. There were two planters in front of each house in the court containing identical shrubs. There was some unused soil around the base of each shrub, and this is where Barbara wanted to plant. My mother never pointed out to her that it was unlikely that anything she planted there would grow. The soil was in poor condition—dirt, in fact—and the shrub would block the sunlight to it. Putting that aside, Mom bought some seeds, and they made a big deal of preparing the area to be planted. They dug a hole, placed the seeds, covered them up, and gave them a good watering. Throughout the course of the day, a few neighbors stopped by to see what was going on and gave Barbara a bit of advice here and there. Mr. Brady watched the entire episode from his porch with interest.

Later that evening, well after all the kids were put to bed for the night, Mr. Brady went around the corner to a vacant lot and found a weed that somewhat resembled the flower Barbara had planted. He didn't think anything of the fact that this particular weed was three feet tall. He returned to the court and proceeded to plant the weed where Barbara had placed her seeds. This was with my parents' consent, of course; they were hysterical over the size of the "flower" he'd chosen but grateful that he thought to do this for Barbara's sake.

The next morning, Mr. Brady, Mom, and Dad were all sitting on the porch waiting for Barbara to wake up and see how her plant had grown. They were excited for her and thought she'd be quite thrilled with her project. Barbara finally woke up and stumbled outside. She took one look at the monster weed, frowned, and didn't say anything. My mother said to her, "Look at your flower! Isn't it incredible! Look at how much it grew!" Barbara replied with a pout, "Yeah, but I didn't want it to grow that fast!" She burst into tears and ran back into the bungalow. You know what they say about best intentions . . .

The Walkers were an elderly couple. Just the two of them and their little white dog, Tinkerbell, lived at the bungalow, but they had six children and dozens of grandchildren who would visit them all summer long. Mr. and Mrs. Walker died on the same day, both of natural causes. I remember the adults in the court always saying how they loved each other so much that one wouldn't be able to live without the other . . . and they were right. Mrs. Walker died in the afternoon and Mr. Walker said to his son, Jimmy, later that night, "I can't live without her." He died just before midnight.

Tom and Eileen (Babs) Kitsen had three sons: Ronnie, Bobby, and Tommy. Their daughter, Eileen, was the youngest. Mr. Kitsen worked for a cruise line, and I remember hearing about all the great vacations they went on.

Mrs. Kitsen had a dog named Rusty. Mr. and Mrs. Kitsen worked during the week and the boys were all grown and worked as well, so Eileen was the only one at home during the day. She was responsible for Rusty. After finishing the morning chores, she figured she was free to go to the beach with Barbara, Mattie, Germaine, Mickey, and his little sister, Barbara Jean. So Eileen would feed the dog, tie him to the porch, and go to the beach . . . and for five hours every day the dog would bark nonstop. Several people complained and the neighbors told Eileen she couldn't leave the dog tied up like that, so she decided the only alternative was to keep the dog locked up in the bungalow.

Upon returning home from the beach the first day of keeping the dog in the house, she found the bottom half of the screen door ripped out. As it turns out, one of the kids on the block mentioned to Eileen earlier that day that he thought he saw Rusty up on the boulevard. Eileen replied, "No. My dog is locked up in the house today." Hah! Little did she know, that *was* Rusty up on the boulevard. So the next day, she went out and found a piece of plywood and nailed it to the bottom half of the screen door so the dog couldn't get out. When she came home that afternoon, she discovered Rusty had managed to escape through the top half of the door. Barbara sat on our porch that afternoon and watched while Eileen, all of thirteen years old, replaced the screen sections of the door.

Eileen finally got smart and closed the solid wood door behind the screen door when she left for the beach the next day. But since she didn't want Rusty to overheat in a stuffy house, she left the windows open. When she came home that afternoon, she found one of the window screens ripped open. The next day, it was a different window screen, and then another, and then another, and another. By the end of the summer, she had replaced every screen in the house and Mr. Kitsen simply couldn't get over how nice and clean the screens had managed to stay that summer.

The Negangasses lived directly across from us. Mr. Negangass was a jolly fellow who reminded me of Buddy Hackett, and while my sister Barbara found little Susan Negangass annoying, Chrissy and I thought she was great fun.

Mrs. Fay had two children from her first marriage and when she married Mr. Fay, he adopted them both. Tommy and Marylou were older than I was and younger than Barbara, so they ran with a completely different crew. I remember I had a crush on Tommy for years. I used to bother him every chance I got, and he would threaten me with kisses if I didn't stop. Of course, I didn't stop.

The families of Hollyhurst were a close-knit group and got along with great ease. When the original families began moving out and others took their place, there were occasional difficulties.

The McDougals had a hard time of it the one and only summer they rented a bungalow in Hollyhurst. They were a young couple, the husband worked in sanitation, with a second job driving a school bus. He lived in the bungalow with his wife, infant daughter, and mother-in-law. One Saturday night after all the kids were in bed, Mr. Brady, Mr. and Mrs. Coogan, and my parents were gathered on the Kitsen's porch where they sipped cocktails and swapped stories late into the evening. There was nothing unusual about this routine—they'd been doing it for years. This particular gathering occurred early in the season, and I guess the McDougals weren't yet up to speed on court society.

According to my mother, sometime after midnight, Mr. McDougal came charging out of his bungalow in his boxer shorts. He was screaming about the noise and that he had a baby sleeping, for Christ's sake. He pushed my father out of his chair, probably because he was the closest, and proceeded to pound him with his fists, screaming the whole time. The other men quickly pulled him off my father and restrained him. This was a robust, young guy and my father was already in his fifties. I can't imagine what he was thinking. They said he was completely out of control. The wife and mother-in-law were terribly embarrassed by his actions that night and wouldn't look anyone in the face afterward. At any rate, not a soul in the court would speak to them the rest of that summer and they were never invited to take part in any court functions. They were blacklisted and didn't return the following year. Barbara told me they moved to another court, and Mom read in the paper a couple of years later that Mr. McDougal was arrested for driving the school bus erratically.

8

TOOTH FAIRY ECONOMICS

Jackie

The summer of 1965 got off to an auspicious start. I must have remembered something of the prior summers because, according to Barbara, I was bouncing around the car for the drive out to Rockaway. It seemed I already had a general grasp of summertime fun at the tender age of three. My parents pulled the car up in front of the court and let us out before they began unloading. Barbara had her hands full with Christine who was only a year and a half old at the time, and with the impatience of a three-year-old, I went tearing into the court toward our bungalow.

When I first began walking, my parents noticed I had a distinctly pigeon-toed gait and my pediatrician prescribed special orthopedic shoes to correct the problem. At some point, I'm pretty sure I had leg braces, although I'm not positive about this, because my parents took all pictures of me from the waist up during that time in an effort to hide this fact from me as I grew older. I was wearing those shoes (and probably those leg braces) as I ran into the court that day, tripped, and sprawled face down on the concrete.

So, instead of having a leisurely day opening up and airing out the bungalow, my parents had to load us back into the car for the drive to Peninsula Hospital, where I had my lip stitched and discovered the loss of my first baby tooth. This incident prompted my introduction to the Tooth Fairy, and during the drive back from the hospital, Barbara told me amazing stories about this generous being and insisted we find my missing tooth so I could put it under my pillow. The accumulation of capital was a foreign concept to me at that point, but I was a clever kid and caught on quickly enough.

When we returned to Hollyhurst, all the neighbors were on hand to fuss over me, but I was interested only in finding that tooth. So, we engaged the services of everyone present and the hunt was on. I don't remember who found the errant tooth, but I placed it under my pillow that night, as per Barbara's instructions. In the morning, I discovered a shiny new quarter for my effort.

Not many three-year-olds are capable of understanding the natural, gradual loss of their baby teeth, and I was no exception. According to

Barbara, I spent the rest of that summer coming up with new ways to knock out my remaining teeth, and I kept a close eye on Christine's dental progression, being under the impression she was too young to mind missing a couple of them.

9

SENSORY MEMORIES

Watercolor painting on a rainy day.—
Jackie, Mom, Dad & Chrissy

There is nothing in the world that can bring you back to a specific time and place as quickly as scent. Our bungalow had its own unique aroma and anyone who has ever had a vacation home—in the mountains or at the shore—understands what I mean. It's most prominent when you first open the house for the season, but it remains there, just not as obvious, and it will sneak up on you when you least expect it.

There are layers to it. At first it's all about mothballs and the staleness that permeates a home that's been uninhabited for months. As you go about cleaning, dusting, and airing out, the house takes on a fresh, clean scent. Then, the beds are made up with linens softened by too many washings and topped with the ever-popular chenille bedspreads, which have a unique bouquet all their own. Every season my mother would purchase a new, colorfully printed oilcloth for the dining table that, when first opened, had an overpowering, synthetic odor that would quickly mellow and blend with the rest. I still use oilcloth for outdoor tables and the scent never fails to remind me of Rockaway. There was the gassy odor of the hot water heater being fired up for the first time, and the musty whiffs from sticky bureau drawers being opened and closed.

But above, beneath, and throughout it all, the house had the unmistakable fragrance of the ocean. The tangy perfume of the salt air was a constant, but you perceived it only at particular moments, like when you crawled into bed for the night or a nap, or when you sat still late in the evening, or when you woke up, especially on chilly, dew-covered mornings. It was always there, the scent of salty air and the sea.

Bungalow living was a casual affair and intentionally arranged to be low maintenance. Linoleum floors, vinyl chairs, iron bed frames, and oilcloth kept things simple and easy to clean. The furnishings were ancient, so you never worried about coffee mug rings on the dressers or tables. When you returned from a day at the beach, you hung the beach towels on the clothesline to dry and in the morning, you grabbed one on your way out. The only thing you had to worry about was getting sand in your bed. As much as you tried to avoid it, it was always there.

My mother would clean the bungalow once a week. She always sent us off to the beach before she started so we wouldn't be underfoot.

She would drop off the linens and clothing at the laundromat and spend the morning emptying the fridge; defrosting the freezer; scrubbing the oven, stove, toilet, and sink; and dusting the shelves and bureaus. Finally, she would open all the windows, turn on the fans, and mop the floor. No one was allowed to enter the bungalow until it was dry. Then she would go outside to tidy up the porch and sweep it clean before she set off to pick up the laundry. How many times did we come running in from the beach onto wet floors while she was still out, and stop in our tracks realizing our transgression? How many times did we grab the mop, erase our sandy footprints, and then sit on the porch like angels to await her return? For us kids, it was summertime, and the living was easy.

We lived outdoors for the most part, weather permitting. There were only five people in my family but there were substantially larger families in many of the other courts. We had several friends who had six, seven or eight siblings. Can you imagine being cooped up with that many people in such a tiny space for an extended period? I can't speak for the others, but my parents were always prepared for the inevitable foul weather. We had shelves full of board games and decks of cards. We also had buckets full of shells we'd collected, and my mother always kept watercolor paint sets on hand. She taught us how to paint scenes onto the giant clamshells the adults used as ashtrays. When the weather was particularly nasty, we stayed indoors huddled around the dining table playing games and listening to the rain drip from numerous roof leaks into the pots and pans my parents strategically placed throughout the bungalow. If it was merely a light rain or sun shower, we could occupy ourselves on the porch with card games, scrabble tournaments, and rounds of Password, our favorite. Frequently, our neighbors would get involved in our games and shout out the answers from their porches. They'd come over and join us when they got tired of yelling. In the evening, after we went to bed for the night, many of the adults would sit on their porches in their rocking chairs and carry on conversations that encompassed the length of the court. We would lie in our beds with the windows open and listen to them discuss whatever the big news of the day was. Sometimes music played softly on the radio, and we fell asleep amidst chirping crickets and the lingering scent of Mr. Duffy's cigar.

10

TRAINS, PLANES, AND AUTOMOBILES

The "El"

As wonderful as this all sounds, I would be remiss if I failed to mention that life in Rockaway came with its own unique quirks. Rockaway Beach has always been an incredibly noisy place.

An elevated railway crosses over Jamaica Bay from Cross Bay Boulevard and travels from Far Rockaway to 116th Street. The "El," as it's called, runs above Rockaway Parkway, which was just down the street from our court. When I was growing up, the CC trains ran about every fifteen minutes, and they had to be the oldest trains in operation in the city. The rail cars had old-fashioned, overhead teardrop handles, prehistoric lighting, and braided wicker seats. My sister Barbara used to have fits because her stockings would catch on the wicker and run. The rail cars were ancient, and it wasn't until the early 1980s that they were finally removed from service. Every time a train came through, the whole house rattled and shook. The noise was overwhelming, and all conversation came to a standstill. We never really noticed the racket unless we had a first-time visitor who would jump out of his or her seat the first time a train rumbled by.

You could get used to the trains; that was easy. The planes were a different matter entirely. JFK Airport is just twenty minutes away by car and Rockaway Beach is directly below the flight path for takeoffs and landings. The planes flew so low over the peninsula you could see their shadows. The bungalow and all its contents would vibrate every time a plane flew overhead, which was every three minutes. Bear in mind, this was before the advent of cable TV, back in the good old days when every TV had an antenna. So, every three minutes, all conversation ceased, and the TV picture turned to snow. You can't imagine how difficult it was to follow the most basic sitcom storyline under these conditions. Then, during the 1970s, the Concord began flying out of JFK. This, not surprisingly, coincided with the widespread use of car alarms. So the Concord took off every day at ten in the morning and again at one in the afternoon and thirty seconds later every car alarm in town went off. We took all of this in stride and would set our watches by the Concord flight schedule. Until the Concord was grounded several years ago, you still could.

The one thing you never got used to were the awful car accidents that occurred down the block on the corner of 101st Street and

Rockaway Parkway underneath the El. These accidents occurred with startling regularity, anywhere from two to four times each week. The El was a hulking, concrete structure with a dark, foreboding presence. The accidents never involved locals because we knew enough to cross under the El only where there was a traffic light. Our corner did not have a traffic light, just a stop sign, so drivers took their life into their hands when they tried to cross. You'd hear the screech of slamming brakes and stop whatever you were doing, your breath escaping through clenched teeth, and seconds later, you'd hear the inevitable crash with its cacophony of crunching metal. Everybody would run out of the court to assist in any way they could while someone called an ambulance. Most of the accidents were fender benders, some were much worse. In minutes, we would be inundated with sirens from every civil service branch in the Rockaways.

What I find amazing, considering what a boisterous place Rockaway could be, was the fact that my parents never had a phone installed in the bungalow, ever. They claimed to enjoy the quiet and didn't want to listen to a ringing phone all summer. Where were they living? At any given moment, there'd be a train going by, a plane flying over, ear-piercing car alarms, sirens blaring, cars crashing, kids crying, and on garbage day, extremely noisy garbage trucks doing their thing. It wasn't until many, many years later I discovered the real reason we never had a telephone at the beach. But we'll get to that later.

11

SPEAKING OF GARBAGE DAY . . .

Taking out the trash

The trash was picked up one day each week and garbage day was as organized as the invasion of the beaches at Normandy. Every bungalow in our court had two or three trash cans stored in the side alley by the shower stall. The court address and bungalow letter were painted on the sides of the cans and on the lids.

Late Tuesday evening, Richie Allen's two boys would come to our court, carry all the trash cans out to the curb and line them up in an orderly fashion. They received tips from each of the court families for this chore. Mr. Murphy, the owner of Hollyhurst, was their uncle and he had set them up with this gig. As soon as we heard the garbage trucks coming up the street, all of the men in residence would stop whatever they were doing and rush out front to oversee the emptying of the cans. You can bet no stray trash would be flying off down the street! When the cans were emptied, the men went to work matching up the lids to the cans and proceed to return all of them to their respective households. Then, two or three of the men would grab their brooms and sweep clean the courtyard and sidewalk. I don't know who instigated this carefully orchestrated operation—it had been going on for as long as anyone could remember—but I have a feeling that my father was involved. The men were on a mission, and it was always a little hectic and exciting for a few moments, and God help us if somebody didn't get the right garbage cans back or a lid didn't fit correctly! Our parents had pride in where they lived and took great care to keep it clean and orderly. After all, the appearance of our court reflected directly on the families who lived there, and these were fastidious, God-fearing people—of Irish descent, of course.

12

BEACH BABIES AND OCEAN DENIZENS

101st Street Jetty

When we were young, one of my parents would accompany us to the beach each day. Since we spent a good chunk of the day there, my parents made sure to have all the gear necessary for such an outing. There were plenty of towels, a couple of chairs, and a giant umbrella. There was a cooler full of food and a couple of large thermoses full of lemonade, iced tea or Kool Aid. There was always a bottle of Dad's special blend tanning lotion—sun block wasn't yet a thing, or if it was, we didn't know about it. There were plenty of pails and shovels, a Frisbee, and a couple of Spalding rubber balls. We played all sorts of games with those balls. They bounced well on the mud and against the boardwalk and were perfect for a round of stickball. Oh, and let's not forget the ubiquitous transistor radio . . . AM only!

My mother always took what she called a "mud chair"—one of those really low beach chairs that sit right on the sand—which she would place at the water's edge where the approaching ripples lapped at her feet. That way, she could keep a close eye on us while we were in the ocean. Quite a few mothers had the same idea, with clusters of them situated along the length of the shoreline.

When it was time for lunch, Mom would shake the sand from the big beach blanket and lay it out under the shade of the umbrella. Then she would take us, one at a time, down to the water and have us rinse off so we were sand free, and she'd carry us back to the blanket so we wouldn't get sand on our feet. She'd wrap us up in a dry towel and give us our lunch, usually a sandwich and a piece of fresh fruit. We were always told that you should digest your food for at least one hour before swimming to avoid cramps, so it was our habit to take a nap after lunch. My mother would take the napkin, aluminum foil and paper cup when I'd finished eating and wipe my face and hands before I'd lie down and fall fast asleep in the shade. I remember so clearly lying there, wrapped in my towel, warm and cozy, with a steady breeze on my face. My nose filled with the scent of the ocean. The sound of the waves breaking and receding and the inconsequential background noise of those around me confirmed my well-being. I fell down into sleep filled with an overwhelming sense of contentment and safekeeping, and upon awakening, knew all was right in my world. What I wouldn't give to experience that sensation just one more time. But, as we all eventually learn, true serenity exists solely within the domain of childhood.

Spending every summer of your life at the beach, you inevitably become comfortable with the ocean and its numerous denizens. East Coast summers are hot, humid, and sticky and you spend as much time in and on the water as possible, simply to stay cool.

We swam in the ocean just about every day and when we weren't swimming, we ambled along the shoreline to discover what the tide washed up. During June, the water temperature was still on the cool side and there generally wasn't much evidence of marine life. Early in the season was the best time to collect shells along the water's edge. When I was a kid, we'd pick up giant conch shells by the dozens. Giant clamshells were another favorite, and the bigger the better, because the adults used them as ashtrays. By mid-July though, the water warmed up substantially, bringing with it a cornucopia of aquatic life forms. At low tide, you could walk up to the jetties, which were encrusted with mussels, starfish, and other creatures. When the conditions were just right, you could spot air holes in the mud at the water's edge and dig for clams. On some days, the clams just washed up with the waves and if you were fast enough, you could scoop up bucketfuls of them. Crabs made their appearance by the end of July, and it wasn't unusual to get pinched while wading. You knew the water was really warming up when the small, clear, harmless jellyfish presented themselves. By August, the water temperature was usually in the mid-seventies to low eighties and that's when the big guns showed up. There was always one week in August when the prehistoric horseshoe crabs made their presence known, crawling from the water's edge and lining the shore by the hundreds, looking for all the world like an invading alien force with their creepy little eyes, spiky stingers, and crabby legs. As a child,

I used to have nightmares about them and trust me, you don't want to step on one while (shudder here) wading.

If horseshoe crabs weren't enough to make your skin crawl, the man-o-war jellyfish—huge, slimy, and blood red—most certainly would. God, they still give me the heebie-jeebies. At times they were legion, making it impossible to swim, and if you were brave enough or hot enough or stupid enough to go in the water, you had to be ever vigilant. I was at the beach one afternoon when a young girl came up for air and her head emerged directly underneath one of those monsters. The lifeguards had a hell of a time cutting that thing off her face. It's incredibly painful to be stung by one and there is nothing more disgusting than having one suctioned to you.

As kids, we would enter the water in groups and arrange our bodies in a circle, facing out, so we could spot when a man-o-war got too close. I bet kids still do that. It's just as bad when they wash up on shore and die, littering the coastline with their stinking, bulbous carcasses.

If the water turned unusually warm in August, there would be a few shark sightings, generally at the most inopportune time. We'd be in the midst of a heat wave and being in the water was the only place to be. On that day, the water would be calm and clear and free of the most offending creatures and feel like heaven on earth. Then we'd hear the shrill of the lifeguard's whistle and look to the tower to see him frantically calling everybody out of the water and signaling "shark" to the other towers with their hands raised over their heads, palms together. We never moved so fast in our lives and long before we hit the sand, the theme from "Jaws" would be playing in our heads. We'd all gather on the shoreline and use our hands to shield our eyes from the sun, standing there hoping to catch a glimpse of the dreaded fin. Fortunately, the sharks only showed up a few times each summer.

There was an abundance of marine life when I was a child. We occasionally spotted giant turtles and, if we were really lucky, whales. One summer, a small whale made its home in Atlantic Beach, just east of Rockaway. It was healthy, unharmed, and seemingly friendly. We knew some of the lifeguards working on those beaches who told us about it. So, our gang made the trip to the bay several times to swim with it. It would swim up alongside us, let us touch it and blow air out of its blowhole. It stayed in Atlantic Beach the whole summer and then one day took off. That was quite an experience.

I'm sorry to report the sea life has dwindled considerably since those days. Today, you're more likely to come across a hypodermic needle than an intact conch shell. Several summers ago, Barbara and her husband Paul were taking a stroll along the beach in Breezy Point. It was a weekday afternoon, and they were the only people on that stretch of beach. Paul saw what he thought was a big fish washed ashore in a wave, and he ran ahead to check it out. It turned out to be the remains of one of the Chinese boat people who had been seeking asylum in this country when their boat floundered in high seas off Rockaway Point. Not exactly what you hope to stumble across while exploring the shoreline. Things have changed considerably, but in the years since, there have still been days when my mother or Barbara would call to let me know that a few horseshoe crabs showed up, or when the man-o-wars had made an appearance. I find myself smiling and shuddering at the news.

13

LOW INCOME HOUSING

(or, The Road to Hell is Paved With Good Intentions)

Vacant lots and the NYC Housing Authority Edgemere Projects

While my sisters and I were busy growing up and running wild along the shore, the Rockaway peninsula was experiencing growing pains of its own.

Between the 1950s and the 1970s, the City of New York, under Mayor Robert Wagner and Mayor John Lindsey, implemented ruthless urban renewal policies that originated with Robert Moses, the notorious Parks Commissioner, and proceeded to destroy hundreds of acres cf prime oceanfront property, and entire communities.

During the 1950s, the New York City Housing Authority built several low-income housing projects in Far Rockaway: Arverne Houses (1951), Hammel Houses (1955), Redfern Houses (1959), and in 1961, it built the Edgemere Houses, which became one of the most brutal housing projects in the city.

Whereas Far Rockaway is just east of Rockaway Park, it was a world apart culturally, socially, and economically. After the introduction of low-income housing, Far Rockaway became a crime-ridden slum and we were warned repeatedly to never, ever go there. With the exception of one reckless foray during my teen years (we'll get to that), the only time I ventured into Far Rockaway was in the relative safety of a car on the way to other points east. For a while, there was an imaginary line between the two towns, but eventually the criminal element stepped over that line and things changed rapidly.

The NYC Housing Authority turned its unwelcome attention to Rockaway Park in the 1960s and during that decade built several more low-income housing projects: Surfside Park (1963), Dayton Beach Park (1964), Beach 105th Street (1966), Dayton Towers (1967), and the Bay Towers (1973). To accomplish that, the NYC Housing Authority bought up, and then tore down, block after block after block of summer bungalows and told thousands of families not to return the next summer. Many of those families—and we knew a lot of them—scrambled to find available bungalows to rent. The vast majority were unsuccessful and left the Rockaways, never to return.

Those ruthless urban policies, and the government officials endorsing them, were responsible for the eradication of entire neighborhoods, replacing them with drab concrete towers surrounded by weedy, vacant lots. The families and businesses that created and shaped those enclaves over generations were displaced, forever obliterating what were once vibrant, unique neighborhoods. There are numerous examples of those ill-conceived strategies throughout New York City, and the decline of the Rockaways is a disturbing example of what damage can be wrought.

14

JOHN THE TURTLE AND HIS FAMOUS DISAPPEARING ACT

John & Susie

The year 1968 was the summer of what we now refer to as "John the Turtle and His Famous Disappearing Act." It seems to me that we always had pet turtles—it was the only pet our parents allowed us to have. They reasoned it was cruel to keep a dog or cat locked up in an apartment all day, and we did live in the city for nine months of the year. So we had turtles, two of them, named John and Suzy, and we had them for years. When we closed up the apartment for the summer, they came with us to the beach. We'd transport them in their clear plastic bowl, complete with island and palm tree, on one of our laps for the drive out to the beach.

One time, John the Turtle came up missing from their bowl. How the story goes depends on whom you ask to retell it.

TAKE ONE: CHRISSY'S VERSION

One summer morning, Chrissy woke to discover John missing from the bowl. She screamed for my mother, crying hysterically, and asked where he could be. Mom told Chrissy he probably just went for a walk. Huh? He climbed out of his bowl, jumped off the tall bedroom bureau, and could be walking around the house? Sure! Mom told us to be very careful walking around the house so we wouldn't step on him. Of course, we believed her. So, for the next week or so, we all tiptoed around the bungalow and my mother would occasionally take a peek under the beds. One afternoon, we were sitting at the table having lunch and Mom claimed to have heard something outside. She got up, opened the screen door, and pronounced, "Look who's back!" as John tried to scramble over the threshold to our surprise and delight. We put him back in his bowl with Suzy and had much discussion about getting a larger bowl and how funny it was that we tiptoed around all this time and he wasn't even in the house.

TAKE TWO: BARBARA'S VERSION

My mother woke up one morning to find John missing from his bowl. Barbara saw her looking into the bowl, which was on top of the kitchen counter, and heard her say, "Now where did he get to?" Barbara went over to investigate and informed Mom that John's fall from the top of the counter would be the equivalent of her falling from the top of the Empire State Building—he wouldn't have survived. Mom told her that John had been climbing out of the bowl for years. He would climb onto Suzy's back, reach up and climb over the edge of the bowl, and drop out of it. He survived the fall off the counter because he was top heavy and would land on his shell. He'd go off exploring for a week or so and eventually turn up when he got hungry. They looked for him but couldn't find him anywhere. When Chrissy and I woke up, Mom informed us that John went for a walk and would eventually show up. We were to be careful where we stepped. A week later, we were sitting at the table eating lunch when John came walking out of my bedroom. He had dust balls clinging to his shell and feet. We cleaned him up, put him back in the bowl with Suzy, and discussed getting them a larger bowl.

TAKE THREE: MOM'S VERSION

My mother woke up one morning to find John missing from the bowl, which sat on top of the TV. She was going about her regular morning ritual when Barbara got up and eventually noticed a turtle missing and informed our mother. Mom looked in the bowl and said, "Looks like John went for another walk." Barbara pointed out that if John somehow got out of his bowl and fell off the TV, he wouldn't have survived. It would be like her falling from the top of the Empire State Building. My mother explained that he would have survived the fall because he was top heavy and would have landed on his shell. Mom told Barbara, "He'll show up when he gets hungry, but take a look around first, see if you can spot him." When Christine and I woke up, she told us that John was out of his bowl taking a walk and to be careful where we stepped. We tiptoed around the house for a week and my mother would occasionally stoop down and look under a bed. About a week later, we were having lunch and my mother got up from the table to go to the kitchen. We heard her exclaim, "There you are!" as she bent over to pick something up off the floor and turned around with John in her hands. We cleaned him up, put him back in the bowl with Suzy, and talked about getting them a larger bowl.

We never did get around to replacing their bowl with a larger one that summer. It became the norm for us to watch where we stepped, and I think my mother found it a good excuse for keeping the hordes of our sandy-footed friends out of the bungalow all summer.

TAKE FOUR: JACKIE'S VERSION

I don't recall any of this, but if I had to guess, I bet one of the turtles died and it would take my mom a few days to get a replacement, hence the story about John taking a walk. While writing this chapter, I told Mom what I thought really happened. She still sticks by her story.

15

SIS

Mom a.k.a. Sis

My mom's name is Rosemary, but everyone called her "Sis." After all, she grew up with four brothers. They all called her that, so I can see how her friends would pick up on that.

As a parent, Mom was tough. *Is* tough (we just celebrated her 99th birthday). The task of disciplinarian fell to her, and we obeyed her orders or paid the price. It did no good to wheedle my father; he gave her free reign in matters concerning us. Growing up, we viewed her tactics as a bit harsh, but since we all ended up successful contributors to the Gross National Product, I must admit the end justified the means in our case.

Christine and I rarely got away with anything because Mom was ALWAYS there. Not only did she know the who, what, when, and where any given day on our social calendar, she would check up on us just to make sure we were where we said we'd be. Her presence was a fact of life and the absolute bane of our existence. If we weren't where we said we'd be, there was hell to pay when we got home. On the other hand, even when she found us exactly where we said we'd be, she invariably caught us doing something we shouldn't have been doing. We never got away with anything. Ever.

Both of my parents were strict, but Mom was the enforcer. Unlike the other nine months of the year, summertime was conducive to leniency, but there were still some things you just didn't mess with. If Mom told you dinner was at five-thirty, you were at the table at five-thirty, and you ate what was put in front of you or you'd end up wearing it. There'd be hell to pay if one of us stayed out past curfew, but Christine would know more about that than I, since she was a regular offender.

There was no excuse for missing Sunday Mass. According to my folks, our failure to attend Mass was a direct reflection on them. I really shouldn't mention that the only time they went to church was for weddings and funerals. When asked why we had to go to Mass but they didn't, we were told, "BECAUSE I SAID SO." Of course, they had a perfectly good excuse for this, but they didn't deign to explain it to us until we were well into adulthood. Apparently, my father had had a previous marriage that ended in divorce and when he married my mother, he was excommunicated from the Catholic Church, as was she for marrying him. Since we never knew of his prior marriage in the first place, it seemed awfully hypocritical to us. You know what they say: What goes around comes around. Since both of my sisters and I ended up divorcing our first husbands, technically, we've all been excommunicated. But you can bet all the grandkids have to attend Mass each week!

Mom wasn't disposed to grounding as a punishment. She realized that having us underfoot all day long would be harder on her than it would be on us. I was never sent to bed without dinner, due to the fact that I was such a picky eater and that would have been more of a reward for me. We didn't have all the toys and electronics kids have today, so there was nothing to take away from us. And the "time-out" hadn't been invented yet. No, Mom was more inclined to give you a quick beating with a belt. It was swift and efficient, and she certainly got her point across. As often as we received the beatings—and we received a lot of them—we were more afraid of her anger than any pain she might inflict. My mom getting mad was a terrifying sight to behold. Christine and I would run into our room with our mother in hot pursuit brandishing my father's black leather belt. We'd dive to the farthest corner of the bed and pull the blankets and pillows over us. Truth be told, we rarely ever sustained a direct hit and we'd end up stifling our laughter because that would just make her angrier. We knew it would be over soon and had no desire to prolong it. You could never call us gluttons for punishment.

My parents wanted the best for us, and in hindsight, that was apparent in all aspects of our upbringing. They did the best they could with what they had at hand, and that included everything from private schools to using the belt. Looking back, I think they did fine. We didn't have much, but we had *everything*, and I consider myself extremely fortunate. Above all else, I will be forever grateful to my parents for providing us the opportunity to fritter away the carefree days of summer in a special place that I will never forget.

16

COMPANY

Mike Gordon, Uncle Tom McCloskey, Aunt Jo Farish,
Cousins Lorraine & Fran Farish, & Barbara

When you have a beach house, it is predestined, you *will* have houseguests. We had a large extended family: My father had seven brothers and sisters, and my mother had four brothers, which meant I ended up with a ridiculous number of first cousins.

We had an unusually close extended family and they all came to visit us during the summer. My parents also had a lot of friends who were frequent guests. Barbara had a ton of friends—I remember boys mostly—and they visited constantly. Every weekend and even during the week, people would drop by for a visit. Now, bear in mind, we never had a phone installed in the bungalow, so most visitors were completely unexpected since they had no way of contacting us. Or so I thought.

This constant barrage of people was a way of life, and considering what little we had, it always amazed me how much there was to go around. I can't figure out if my mother was psychic or just knew how to stretch food. She had the ability to make two loaves and four fishes into a meal for the masses. I'm not kidding. On any given summer weekend, an extra half dozen people would show up at our door and my mother, being the gracious hostess she was, provided. Period. Within minutes—it seemed like minutes, to me—massive amounts of food would magically appear on the table.

She always served buffet style and everyone helped himself. Giant casseroles of baked ziti with sausage, or lasagna, or spaghetti and meatballs would materialize along with an antipasto platter, a huge salad, and fresh, hot, Italian bread. I guess it's possible she kept a stash of meatballs in the freezer, but our freezer was the size of a football and if you wanted to get anything out of it, you could spend days chipping away at the ice encrusting it. Keep in mind, this was well before every home had a microwave oven. The fact is, Mom bought and cooked everything fresh; I don't think she had the time or inclination to freeze vast amounts of food, even if there had been room for it.

She pulled this off repeatedly over the years and not just with Italian food. There was the ever-popular corned beef and cabbage, the huge trays of cold cuts for sandwiches, and the platters piled high with pancakes or French toast. Don't ask me where those enormous kettles of clam chowder came from.

In the years since, I've tried to emulate Mom's ability to be ready for anything. But even now with my gigantic sub-zero fridge, double oven, six-burner stovetop, and library of Martha Stewart books, I'm still caught off guard when people show up unexpectedly. I've concluded this is a talent one is born with. You either have it or you don't. Mom had it.

We had to be prepared for anything living at the beach, and believe me, just about anything could and would happen. One day during the summer of 1969—I know it was a weekday because my father was at work—quite a crowd show up. Uncle Mickey and his girlfriend, Isabelle (soon to become Aunt Isabelle), and my mother's great friend, Gertie Toomey, and her two kids were there, among other visitors. We would hang a sign on the door that said, "At the Beach," and everyone knew we went to the beach on 101st Street. Throughout the day, several more friends showed up there.

At some point in the afternoon, the sky turned dark, the wind picked up, and the lifeguards called everyone out of the water. We frantically grabbed our beach gear and headed back to the bungalow under threatening skies static with lightning, booming with thunder, and filled with the scent of ozone. We barely made it back to the house before the heavens opened up. Just as all sixteen of us crammed into the bungalow, all hell broke loose. Hail the size of golf balls hammered on the roof, lightning flashed, and the wind howled. We'd battened down the hatches and were trying to make ourselves comfortable, but our tiny bungalow was never meant to have that many people in it at the same time. Naturally, the power went out.

When the power goes out in Rockaway, you never know when it will come back on, so our thoughts turned at once to the refrigerator. Everyone knows it's a mortal sin to waste food. so there was only one thing to do: Eat it all. Immediately. My mother turned her attention to cooking and serving the entire contents of the fridge. Somebody decided the storm was as good an excuse as any for a party and began mixing up cocktails.

We had a high old time inside while the storm raged outside. That is, until the ice cubes ran out. I remember my mother's face when she opened the freezer for more ice: Her mouth formed a giant O. No electricity, no ice cubes. Then I practically saw the light bulb go on over her head. She grabbed a pail, went out to the porch and scooped up as much of the hail as she could. Cocktails, anyone? The hail was a foot deep on the porch and the party sailed on.

When the storm had passed, a group of us walked to the boardwalk to survey the damage. Car windshields were cracked, power lines were down, and dozens of birds lie dead. The flowerbeds along Shorefront Parkway were decimated and the shoreline was littered with driftwood and whatever else the ocean had coughed up that afternoon.

About six o'clock, my father arrived home from work. Unaware of the storm because the weather had been clear in the city, you could tell he didn't believe our tale of destruction at first. The sun was out, and the evidence had melted off the porch. Mom ran to the freezer, where she'd thought to save some hail as proof. But either it had melted, too, or someone had used it to chill a cocktail. And although there were sixteen witnesses, some of us had consumed copious quantities of liquor. People told that story for years and years and years.

It never ceases to amaze me how many people could sleep under our roof at one time. My parents had a queen size bed and a day bed/trundle in their room. Our room had a double bed and a huge old-fashioned crib. It was more like a small bed with a footboard, a headboard and side railings, and because Christine was always so tiny, I think she slept in it until she was about twelve years old. Barbara and I shared the double bed until she got married. The main room was furnished with a dining table and chairs, a day bed/trundle, two overstuffed easy chairs, the TV stand, and the refrigerator.

My Uncle Ed, Aunt Ruth, and their three daughters, Caroline, Maryann, and Dorothy, came to visit us in Rockaway many times over the years. They lived in upstate New York, so when they visited, they always stayed over. Christine's diminutive size was not the norm in my family; most everyone else was of standard size and quite a few were substantially larger. My parents segregated us by sex, so the men slept in my room with the double bed and the crib, and the women slept in my parents' room with the double bed and trundle and on the trundle in the living room. Dad and Uncle Ed in one room was reasonable; eight females in three beds was ridiculous. Being the youngest, Christine and I thought it was a great adventure, though it must have been terribly uncomfortable for everyone else. With the snoring blaring in stereo from the other bedroom, I find it hard to believe any of us could have gotten much shut eye. The whole court had to be sleep deprived with that racket.

The summer months delivered a continuous stream of visiting friends and family. Friends of Barbara's or my parents' friends, like Pat Vitale or Eddie Eustace, would stop by. In later years, my own friends would come out from the city. My parents wouldn't hear of anyone driving back to the city or staying in a hotel; we would make room. Believe me when I say there was nothing unusual about getting up in the morning and seeing Pat sprawled on an easy chair in the living room, or Barbara's latest beau shivering on a chaise lounge on the porch, or Mr. Eustace curled up—and I mean CURLED up—in the crib! Snoring. LOUDLY. I'm not making this stuff up.

No matter how many people showed up, or how many mouths there were to feed, or whatever the weather brought down on us, we always made do, and let me tell you something: It was always fun.

17

FLAGS

Gene Sullivan and Dad in Frumpkin's Court

Rockaway Beach was a predominantly Irish neighborhood and if you didn't know that before you arrived, you would have no doubt of it by the time you left. If the family surnames and business names or the overflowing attendance at Sunday mass escaped you, the ubiquitous green, white, and orange flags would clue you in.

Flags were everywhere. American flags flew from the firehouse, the post office, the police station, and from just about every other building in town. Almost every bungalow in every court sported an American flag and, right alongside it, the flag of Ireland. So, every house had at least two flags, and if there were fifty bungalows in a court, there would be at least one hundred flags flapping in the breeze. Just to be on the safe side, the bungalows with street frontage would fly an extra-large flag or two, and on holidays yet more flags were unfurled. Every bar and restaurant flew its share of both flags, and towering flagpoles were erected throughout town with impunity. Not to mention, we had mini flags on our bicycles and car antennas. Rockaway was a flag-happy town and especially on a windy day, all those flags created quite a racket.

People took their flag etiquette seriously back then. The first person up in the morning would put out the flags. You didn't have your coffee or read the paper until the colors were flying. You never flew the flags during inclement weather, and God forbid you weren't home when it started to rain to bring them in. One of your neighbors would take care of it and be sure to point out that favor when you arrived home, at which time you would thank him or her profusely.

Flags were taken down at dusk unless there was sufficient artificial illumination. When a flag started to fray at the edges or look a little dingy, it would be burned, as tradition and etiquette demands. It was always a little sad when a flag accidentally fell or touched the ground because then too it would have to be burned. You didn't use a flag as a tablecloth, and you didn't let little kids carry them around as blankies because then they'd have to be burned, as well. Burning the flag was a solemn occasion, and the men of our court would stand at attention and hold their right hands over their hearts during the execution. Many of them were veterans and took their allegiance to our national symbol seriously. It's been a long, long time since I've witnessed an honorable flag burning. I wonder if this is yet another American tradition that has fallen by the wayside.

We went through a lot of flags over the years.

18

FRIENDS AND ENEMIES

Karen Holzwarth & Jackie

I never really picked out the people who became my friends. My younger sister, Christine, picked them for me. Chrissy was always much more outgoing than I was, and it didn't matter where we were or what the setting was, she always found friends for us. Whether we were on vacation in the Poconos or Florida or Norfolk or upstate New York, we would go to the gathering place for kids, and I would mope around and wait until Chrissy brought over our new friends and introduced me. She's only a year and a half younger than I am, and since she was so good at making friends and I wasn't, we always ran in the same crowd. That's the way it always was, and it was never more evident than in Rockaway.

During the summer of 1970, we met two girls who would become our best and longest Rockaway friends. Karen lived in Rockaway year-round, and I thought she was the luckiest kid on the planet to live in the paradise that was ours for only three glorious months each year. For a seven- or eight-year-old, it just didn't get any better than that.

Karen's mother, Joanie, was divorced. Karen never talked about her father, and we never asked. I remember that every few years they moved to a different place and, of course, I found that awfully exciting and exotic. Karen's grandmother, Nana, lived around the corner from our bungalow on Rockaway Beach Boulevard. Regardless of where Karen's current home was, she invariably spent the summer at Nana's. Every Memorial Day weekend my parents would load the houseplants and us kids into the car and head out to Rockaway to open up the bungalow for the season, and as soon as the house was opened and the car unpacked, Chrissy and I would race around the block to call on Karen. We had established our own summer rituals and I wonder if she looked forward to it as much as we did.

Our other best friend was Karen's cousin, Rosemary. It was always "Rosemary;" we never shortened her name to "Rosie," "Rose," or "Ro." We pronounced it "RoseMARY." I don't know why, but that's how we pronounced it. Rosemary was the only kid I knew growing up who had braces. What I didn't understand back then was that she was from Scarsdale, and being from Scarsdale, she could afford braces. I mean, I knew she lived someplace called "Scarsdale." She was always telling everyone where she was from. But at the time, I didn't understand it was *Scarsdale.*

Rosemary's parents would pack her up and drop her off at Nana's for the entire summer each year. Her father was a judge. Again, being a kid, I didn't really understand what it meant to have a father who was a judge. Of course, everybody in Rockaway knew what he did for a living and where they lived. That was our fault, because whenever we'd meet new kids, we always introduced her as RoseMARY, she lives in Scarsdale, and her father is a judge. So, RoseMARY got to spend her summers slumming with us.

Barbara was another great friend of ours. Still is. She lived on 118th Street and was a year-round resident. Still is. As with many of the good Irish families of Rockaway, she had a brother who was a priest, a vocation held in high regard by everyone. But Barbara possessed something else that was even more sacrosanct: an older sister who saw the Beatles at Shea Stadium! Barbara's sister had a treasure trove of cool Beatles paraphernalia, and we used to hang out at their house going through it while listening to her records—that is, when her sister wasn't around. At some point, we concluded that we were related by marriage via some second cousin twice removed of my father's, who was married to the great-aunt of Barbara's mother's brother-in-law. Or something like that. It didn't matter: from that point on we introduced ourselves as cousins.

Tara was another member of our crew during the summers she spent in Rockaway. She lived up the block from us in Callahan's Court and in Riverdale in the Bronx the rest of the year. She was taller than the rest of us but took a long time to "develop," so her nickname was "Titless Tara." That nickname followed her around well after it no longer applied.

Maureen, another year-round resident, lived around the corner from us in a house on 102nd Street until her family moved to the Bay

Towers. She lived next door to Karen at the time. She had three brothers: Tommy, Billy, and Jimmy. Jimmy was part of our crowd even after Maureen stopped hanging out with us. When she started high school, she made new friends, but we still saw her around. I dated Billy for a while. Jimmy was such a sweet kid. When we were growing up, his dream was to have his own deli. Years later, he realized his goal with a shop located on 109th Street. I guess it wasn't all it was cracked up to be because I heard that he later became a court officer.

Liz was another Bronx girl who summered in a court on 109th Street. Liz was tall, blonde, blue-eyed, and freckled, and she was the funny one in our gang.

Chris lived in Callahan's Court and was from the Bronx, too. We probably knew Chris before any of our other friends. The Fraziers and Callahans were cousins and since we lived on the same block, our families had known each other for years. Chris always wore his blond hair long, hanging over his face. With his freckles and sunny disposition, you could easily mistake him for a California grom. He had an older brother, Billy, and two older sisters, Susy and Ginger. Susy was lithe, pretty, and sweet. Ginger was our own personal tormentor.

Maura lived around the corner from us, but we could cut through another court to get to her house. She had something like nine brothers and sisters, and I had the biggest crush on her brother, Patrick, but after a few years, they stopped coming to Rockaway for the summer and we never heard from them again. I was about ten years old and completely devastated.

Monica lived next door to us in Cynthia Court when we were very young—five, six, and seven. She was an exceptionally sweet and pretty little girl with a cute older brother named Owen, with whom we were all in love. When Owen would come around, all the girls would giggle and get shy, and he would chase us and try to kiss us. It was during the summer of 1970 that my parents took Christine, Monica, and me to Palisades Park for the day. It was one of those wonderful summer days that live in the minds of children forever. We were fortunate to have gone when we did because Palisades Park closed its doors for good in 1971.

Over the years, our friends came and went. We knew just about everyone on the peninsula, if not directly, then through our parents or older sister or other court residents. There were quite a few people my parents didn't want us running around with for various reasons. I remember one family that lived in another court on our block. I think there were five siblings, and we became friends with the two who were our age. Their father had a speech impediment and he always called his son Anthony, "Antny." Not surprisingly, we all called him "Antny," too. Anthony hated that. It never fails to amaze me how cruel we could be. But the speech impediment is not why my parents didn't want us around them. In spite of the fact they were not as well off as the rest of us, they weren't bad. My mother didn't want us around them on account of their personal hygiene standards—or I should say, lack thereof. Whenever we were with them, we inevitably came home incessantly scratching our heads. They had a perpetual case of head lice. My mother would spot us scratching and ask if we'd been hanging out with those kids again. We would admit to running into them and she'd go running for the benzene hex chloride and lice comb. That comb was a torture device and after several embarrassingly tearful sessions on the porch, in full view of the neighbors, we needed no further reminders to keep our distance.

Another family we were told to steer clear of was the Dennehys. There seemed to be about a dozen siblings covering all the age groups.

Everybody had at least one dreadful Dennehy experience. If I saw them walking in my direction on the street, I would run across the street and into a store to avoid them. There was no safety in crowds either. If they came upon a group of kids hanging out, they would instinctively pick out the weakest and proceed to torment that individual mercilessly. They resembled a pack of wolves in that respect.

Once, I came upon them on the boulevard, right in front of St. Camillus Church. Before I knew it, they were on me. Four or five of them were grabbing and pinching and pulling my hair right there in the middle of the street in broad daylight. I was only nine or ten, scared to death, and started screaming and crying. A passing car stopped, scaring them off. I ran home in tears. It was probably the most traumatic experience of my life up until then.

Whenever there was an especially high tide, the water in Jamaica Bay would rise so dramatically that you could "safely" jump off Cross Bay Bridge into the bay. It was still a long way down and I never considered doing it, but there was always a handful of kids who couldn't ignore the dare. Sometime in the late 1970s, a group, including a few members of the Dennehy tribe, was on the bridge taking turns diving into the bay. Rumor has it they were drinking. Some say a gust of wind blew one of the Dennehy boys into a concrete piling. In any event, it took four or five days for what was left of his crab-eaten body to wash up. I don't know anyone who mourned him. We didn't care. All we knew was that there was one fewer Dennehy to deal with. A few years later, I heard from a friend that one of the other brothers shot himself. Make that two down.

What would summer be without a major crush or two? I've had more than my fair share over the years and for the most part that's what they remained. I was pretty lame when it came to boys.

In our neighborhood, the crew you ran with was based on age. The youngest group, anywhere in age from seven to eleven, hung out in the Love Box located on 101st Street. The middle group consisted of kids from about twelve to sixteen and they hung out on the corner in front of Allen's Deli, also on 101st Street. The older group, anyone seventeen and up, hung out in the park on 109th Street. These were the meeting places for the evening activities.

The groups would change each summer, adding or dropping people, and there were always rival groups of the same age, whom we referred to as either the bad kids or the goody-two-shoes. We always thought of ourselves as somewhere in-between. If another group would get to those respective hangout spots first, your squad would have to make do elsewhere and would generally end up at the boardwalk.

In spite of our age-consciousness, we all knew each other since our worlds overlapped at the beach and parties, and in the courts in which we lived. Since I depended on my sister Chrissy to make friends for me, I was always the oldest in my crowd. That could be good, and it could be bad. In many ways, I was the leader, and for the most part, they deferred to my advanced years and experience. When it came to mischief, however, Chris was the pied piper and nothing I could say or do would dissuade the others from following her lead.

Our crew included a number of boys over the years: Chris, Tommy, Ronnie, Jimmy, Patrick, and others who came and went over the years whose names I can't recall. They were all younger than I was and, therefore, beneath my notice. Besides, they all had eyes for Christine. The guys in whom I was interested were a little older and out of my reach, as they ran with an older crowd.

Maura was one of my best friends, and I was eight or nine years old when I had my first summer crush on her older brother, Patrick. He had a smooth, tan complexion, the bluest of blue eyes, and always wore his brown hair in a crew cut. Naturally, Maura knew how I felt about him because that's all I ever talked about. Once, I talked her into giving me a kiss because I thought that's what it would be like to kiss her brother! He was a year or two older than I was and ran with a group of boys who would occasionally hook up with our gang. When we combined groups, we would have enough people to play our favorite games on a large scale. Ringalario, Red Light, Green Light, Run, Catch & Kiss, Giant Step, and Hide and Go Seek, to name a few. When we played one of the hiding games, I always tried to hide near Patrick. If he was "it," I always let him find me.

It was during one of those games that I became aware he felt the same way about me. We were playing Ringalario and both Patrick and I were hiding on the same porch. I was crouched behind the railing in the bushes, and he was directly across from me underneath a bench. We were very quiet so we couldn't be found. I wanted to stay there forever! Out of nowhere, he asked me if I wanted to go out with him! OH MY GOD! My heart was in my throat, and I'd apparently lost my mind because I said, "Um, I don't know. I'll have to make sure it's OK with your sister."

DUH!!! I was such a GEEK! The moment the words left my mouth I knew I'd lost my chance, and I avoided him the rest of that summer. Maura's family didn't return to the beach the following year and I never saw her or Patrick again. I still haven't forgiven myself for my stupidity. This was the first of many wasted opportunities when it came to boys. It's no wonder I was a virgin until . . . never mind.

19

WHEN HARRY MET BARBARA

Harry Denny & Barbara

During the summer of 1970, my sister, Barbara, began dating her future husband. Barbara was a true child of the 50s—which I consider to have been the final decade of genuine innocence in this country. Every aspect of her life and personality was a reflection of the era in which she grew up. She was Daddy's little princess. She had no thoughts of college or career. As much as my mother tried to talk her out of getting married so young, that was Barbara's objective. And she did exactly that. She became engaged on the day she graduated from high school, was married the following year, had her first child nine months later, and her second child twenty-two months after that. To be a wife and mother was the life she always dreamed of.

Barbara was a clever individual for the most part, but on the odd occasion, she failed to think things through. She decided to bring her boyfriend out to Rockaway one summer day to meet some of the family.

So, Barbara showed up one afternoon with this guy, Harry Denny, from Brooklyn of all places. I don't think I'd ever met anyone from Brooklyn at that point. He was a year ahead of her in high school and his sister, Patty, who was in Barbara's class, introduced them. They had gone out on a number of dates and from what we could tell, he was a fairly conservative individual. He took her to nice restaurants, brought her home on time, and was always well mannered.

Initially, he was supposed to come by just for the afternoon, but the day got away from them, and before anyone realized it, it was evening, and everybody had consumed quite a few drinks. My mother told Barbara he shouldn't drive home and could spend the night at our place.

As usual, we had a few other houseguests that particular weekend. My mother's brothers, Mickey and Gooch, and my godfather, Pat Vitale, were there. Later that evening, they all sat down for a game of poker with Mr. Kitsen and Mr. Brady.

Harry had a few drinks and lurched off to bed around 10:00 p.m. A little after midnight, Harry stumbled out of the bedroom, disoriented and still a bit tipsy. Apparently, he needed to relieve himself and he staggered into the living room where the poker game was still in full swing. Much to my mother's distress, he was clad only in his briefs.

This was one of my mother's first experiences with her future son-in-law and she was more than a little alarmed at his state of undress, which, I might add, he didn't really seem to notice. Didn't he realize with whom he was dealing? We were a bunch of repressed Irish Catholics! We didn't walk around undressed in front of each other, much less around total strangers! My mother stared at him in disbelief as he made his way to the bathroom and back to bed again. Her brothers teased her relentlessly with a steady commentary on how they'd heard this Harry was such a nice, upstanding guy. He was certainly upstanding at that point!

The next morning, while having coffee together, my mother informed Barbara of Harry's midnight stroll to the bathroom the night before. She was pretty embarrassed but nowhere near as embarrassed as Harry was when told of his behavior. He turned a violent shade of red and apologized profusely to my mother. As our various guests made their appearance that morning, he proceeded to apologize to each and every one numerous times. His blush had finally receded when Uncle Mickey came in and said to Harry, "Oh, good morning, I didn't recognize you with your clothes on."

Harry was so distraught that Mom finally took pity on him. She opened the screen door to the porch, where Gooch was passed out on a chaise lounge, snoring at the top of his lungs, clad only in his boxers. "Don't worry about it, Harry. Consider yourself part of the family."

I think that was the weekend my father finally loosened his death grip on his eldest daughter. If she was going to leave the nest, he figured she'd be safe with Harry. So Harry got my parents' approval to keep pursuing my sister and the following year they became engaged.

20

BEACH DAZE

Chrissy, Mom, Jackie

By eight or nine years of age, once we were old enough to cross the street by ourselves, we were no longer dependent on our parents to go to the beach. Christine and I would roll out of bed in the morning, put on our bathing suits, slide into our flip-flops, grab our towels and head out. We never bothered with beach chairs, umbrellas, or food. Surely, later in the day one of my parents would show up with all that stuff. We never locked the front door, so we didn't even have to carry a key. We truly didn't have a care in the world and the most pressing matter was to get the sand beneath our feet and dive headfirst into a wave.

Every day at the beach was the same in many ways, but you never knew what surprises the ocean would bring. You didn't know what the tide was like until you saw it. Some days, the high tide would hurl monster waves along the coastline and practically obliterate the beach. Other days, the tide would be so low it felt like you had to walk a mile to the surf and another mile for water only knee deep.

Sometimes sandbars would form and the moment you hit the boardwalk and looked out over the ocean, you knew it. You could tell by the way the swimmers were dispersed. A group of people would be off by themselves—a substantial distance from the shore—and a large gap of water would separate them from all the other swimmers. They'd be much further out but the water would only be up to their ankles or knees. Sandbars were always such a strange phenomenon. They really could give one the impression people were walking on water out in the middle of the ocean. Predictably, a bunch of smaller kids would try to make their way out to the sandbar.

Sandbars were great fun because they entailed swimming out "over your head" to reach them. We were all exceptional swimmers, but it was always a little scary when your feet lost touch with the bottom, and if we weren't brave enough to swim out by ourselves, we'd stand there yelling and waving our arms hoping someone would give us a hand getting out there. Sandbars generally lasted only a couple of days. They were precarious formations and you didn't want to be on one when it began deforming. I vividly recall a group of swimmers having to be rescued when the sandbar on which they stood collapsed beneath them. I remember standing at the water's edge watching all those people, most of whom I knew, flailing wildly while the lifeguards went about pulling them onto shore, sometimes two at a time, and then running back in to rescue more. Every one of them survived.

21

SOMETIMES HAVING A BIG SISTER IS A GOOD THING

Sandcastle—Chrissy, Jackie, Terry, Barbara Jean & Mickey

When we were younger, Barbara and her friends used to take Chrissy and me into the water "over our heads." They were older and taller, had their feet firmly planted, and we'd have our arms around their necks, strangling them, holding on for dear life. The guys would lift us over their heads and toss us way up in the air and we could only hope they'd be close when we surfaced. Then they would dunk us until we screamed UNCLE! All in all, generally scaring the shit out of us.

Then they'd put us on their shoulders, and we'd have "chicken fights." The whole object of a chicken fight was to knock your opponent off the other person's shoulders. Sometimes it was just between two kids and other times there'd be four, five, or six of us going at it all at once. The last person still atop someone's shoulders was the winner. Chicken fights were always a no-holds-barred, free-for-all and Chrissy, scrappy kid that she was, was particularly vicious at that game.

Barbara's friends were always a ton of fun. Sometimes, you'd be sitting or lying on your towel, minding your own business, and suddenly a couple of them would grab you by the arms and legs. They'd carry you down to the water as fast as they could and then swing you back and forth as high as possible and fling you into an oncoming wave. You'd think this would be a lot of fun. But unfortunately, it generally took place on those days you didn't want to be in the water, for any number of reasons, from cold temperatures to nasty jellyfish. So, from the moment they grabbed you, you'd fight like crazy to get free, and everybody on the beach would watch the ensuing scene, cheering on and encouraging the protagonists. You didn't necessarily want to fight too hard, because if you managed to free up one of your appendages, you'd end up being dragged to the water's edge. Ouch. This doesn't really sound like fun, does it? It was, though. We all knew to put up just enough of a fight to make it look good, but not enough to cause any damage. As you dragged your sodden self back up the sand, you'd receive a round of applause for being a good sport.

Once, when Christine was seven or eight, Tommy Kitsen scooped her up out of the sand and ran down to the water's edge with the intent of throwing her in. Chris was such a tiny kid, so it took only one person to accomplish that task. For whatever reason, she was not in the mood to be dumped in the water and made this abundantly clear when she bit Tommy on the wrist. I mean, she really bit into him—breaking the skin. It was painful enough that Tommy dropped her like a hot potato. My mother witnessed the whole thing from her beach chair and she was pissed. Chrissy had a terrible biting habit growing up and you'd think she'd have outgrown it by that age. Apparently not. Tommy ended up going to the hospital to get a tetanus shot and I don't recall Chrissy ever being thrown in the water again.

The older kids were always especially nice to Chrissy and me, being Barbara's younger sisters. They generally thought us younger kids were annoying, but there were enough times they went out of their way to be nice to us and I remember them all fondly. Sometimes, one of us would be placed in the center of a big beach blanket and the guys would grab the edges of the blanket on all sides. They'd count, "One! Two! Three!" and then lift up the blanket, tossing us high into the air again and again. It was fun and it was scary and we'd each take our turn, laughing and screaming our heads off.

One fine summer day, Chrissy and I were attempting to build a sandcastle at the water's edge and before we knew it, a half dozen of Barbara's friends came over and began to help us. We spent a good portion of the day on that project and when we deemed it complete, everybody on the beach came down to inspect it. It was huge! It was so impressive my mother ran back to the bungalow to get her camera. Whenever I come across that photo, that day comes back to me in a flash, and I remember feeling terribly self-important as I gave instructions to my "helpers" to build up walls here and there, and to go get buckets of water, all the while demonstrating the fine art of "dripping." It was a terrific sandcastle.

22

HOW TO ENHANCE YOUR ALLOWANCE

(without really trying)

Some of my parents generous friends: Rita Degnan, Roman Alvarez,
Pat Vitale, Peggy McShea on the Boardwalk

My parents were frugal when it came to money. After all, we are part
Irish, and historically speaking, my people are known to be tightfisted.
My sisters and I were given a weekly allowance, but it came with a
price. We had to do a few minor chores around the house—nothing
major, mind you. On Saturday mornings, we straightened up our room
and did a little light dusting and vacuuming. Our apartment in the city

wasn't large and the bungalow was downright tiny, so all in all, we got off easy.

Still, a couple of bucks wasn't much to work with. So, whenever the opportunity arose to earn a few dollars more, we welcomed it. We couldn't get our working papers until we were thirteen, so we really had to scrounge around for additional funds before we reached that magic age. For instance, when we visited my cousins who lived in upstate New York, we would maybe rake leaves or shovel snow off the driveway. There was the occasional babysitting gig, but nothing on a regular basis. When there was a poker game, we could earn tips serving sandwiches, snacks, and drinks. And yes, I knew how to pour a glass of beer properly and exactly how much foam was acceptable.

However, at a young age, my sisters and I discovered other means of acquiring capital that required little or no exertion whatsoever. As it turned out, most of my parents' closest friends, the ones whom they saw on a regular basis, were childless. My godfather Pat Vitale had never married. Barbara's godfather Dominic Daniello and his wife Emily never had children. Roman Alvarez was another single guy. Barbara's godmother Peggy McShea never married. Etc., etc., etc. Granted, they had many friends who did have children, but I don't recall spending anywhere near as much time with them. Whether they were getting together in the neighborhood, vacationing together, or attending social functions, generally speaking, we were the only kids in attendance. I guess that would be considered strange these days. But hey, that was our experience and there were definitely some advantages.

My sisters and I were brought up with strict manners and whenever we encountered any of my parents' friends, we were always polite.

Upon greeting them, we would give them each a hug and kiss hello During this process, without fail, each of them would slip us a couple of bucks. Some of them would slide it into the palm of our hand much the way you would to a maitre'd before being seated. Others would do it on the sly, stashing it in a shirt or jacket pocket and pretending nothing was happening, as if it was a big secret or something. Still others would make a big production out of it, digging into their pocket or purse and brandishing the bills in the air to make sure everyone knew what was going on. Some were more generous than others. Pat was always good for a five spot, which was a lot of money to a ten-year-old back then. But mostly, it was one or two dollars apiece. No matter, we always appreciated it. And hey, it could add up fast.

There was a local bar and restaurant in the city called The Fireside in which the adults hung out on Saturday afternoons to watch the horse races on TV and do a little recreational wagering on the side. Chris and I would make a point of stopping in on our way to or from the park. My parents always sat at the end of the bar in the back, farthest from the front door. This was serendipitous for us since we had to stop and greet all the patrons along the length of the bar, hugging, kissing, and pocketing the loot along the way. Shoot, we even stopped in when we knew our parents weren't there! Okay, maybe we were on the make, but it sure beat any type of manual labor. They enjoyed it, we enjoyed it, and so what if someone pinched your cheeks a little too hard or someone smelled a little funny. Maybe they thought we were cute, maybe they thought we needed to be fattened up—they were always telling us to go and buy some candy. Whatever the case, they gave us cash and we were grateful.

It was a similar scenario in Rockaway. We always enjoyed it when Mom and Dad's generous friends came to visit. They were always welcome. Hell, we lived three blocks from Playland and the Midway. We needed some form of income to buy ice cream and cotton candy, play the games, and go on all the rides!

23

HURRICANE AGNES

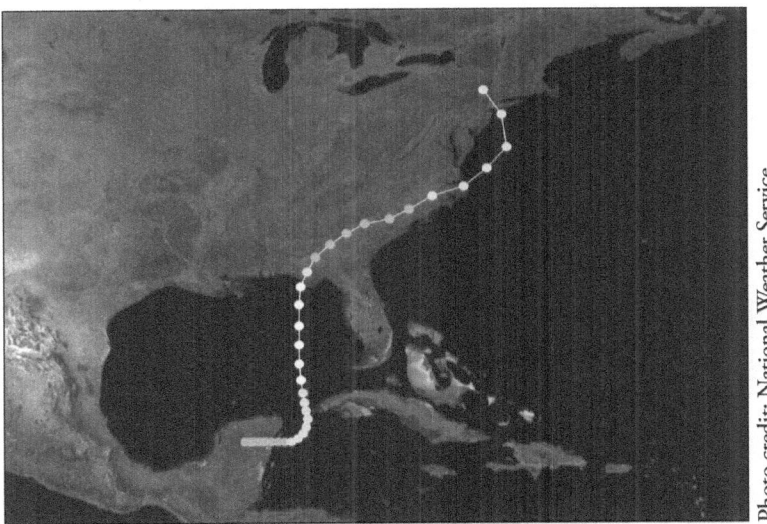

Photo credit: National Weather Service

The Track of Hurricane Agnes

The summer of 1972 began with a bang. We had only just arrived in Rockaway for the season when Hurricane Agnes came roaring up the eastern seaboard in late June. Hurricane Agnes was one of the costliest natural disasters in history causing over two billion dollars in losses. Two billion dollars was worth a lot more than it is today. One hundred and twenty-two deaths were attributed to Agnes, twenty-five of them in New York State.

The weather service suggested evacuation of the Rockaway peninsula, but it wasn't mandatory. Those who stayed were preparing for the worst and nailing down anything that moved. I remember the men in our court working together to board up all the windows. Porch furniture and trashcans were brought inside, and every available bucket, bottle, and jar was filled with water. The water heaters were turned off and gas lines were shut down. My parents bought extra candles, batteries, and ice for the coolers and we stocked up on food that didn't need to be refrigerated. Being the ten-year-old that I was, I found it exciting because it was so scary.

I remember Agnes well because the worst of the storm hit Rockaway on a Friday night, and Friday night was poker night in Hollyhurst court and the men of Hollyhurst weren't about to let little old Agnes interrupt their weekly poker game. Uh-uh. It was one of those storms where the bay, quite literally, met the ocean. The rainfall was so tremendous that the entire peninsula was under water. I remember huddling in the living room with my sisters, listening to the howling wind. At times we could feel the whole house shake and I thought the roof would be torn off just like in The Wizard of Oz.

So, you can imagine our surprise when we saw my father preparing to go outside. We begged him not to and held onto him, fearing he would be swept up into the hurricane. He made light of it and told us not to worry, it was only twenty feet to Mr. Duffy's porch. I noticed my mother didn't seem to be the least bit concerned. He grabbed the big, striped, beach umbrella as my mother prepared to open the door. The screen door slammed open. Dad opened the umbrella up only half-way, and we stood in the doorway and watched as he battled the wind and rain for the twenty-foot walk to Mr. Duffy's door. We were relieved that he arrived unscathed but then we saw that Mr. Brady was stranded on his own porch and was yelling for my father to come and get him. So, Dad made his way to the Bradys' bungalow to collect Frank who grabbed hold of the umbrella as well and together they battled their way back to the Duffy's. I think I held my breath the whole time and when they were safely inside, we all cheered.

I tried valiantly to stay awake that night in case Dad needed help getting back home, but the excitement was too much for me and I was tucked snuggly in bed by the time the game ended. Dad was at the table the next morning, but I never got around to asking him who the big winner was that night.

24

MY SISTER, THE WIFE

Uncle Tom McCloskey, Barbara & Harry Denny

My sister Barbara was born in 1954 and, for all intents and purposes, was of a different generation than Christine and me. She's eight years older than I am and just short of ten years older than Chrissy. Our numerous first cousins are closer in age to Barb than we are. They have a shared childhood bond Chrissy and I never really experienced, showing up late for the party as we did.

Big changes were in store for our family in the summer of 1973. Barbara was married in mid-June, and it was the first summer she wasn't with us in the car when we left for the beach.

Our little bungalow suddenly seemed roomier, and while Christine and I were thrilled at having more drawer and closet space, we felt her absence in a hundred little ways each day. I missed her rocking on the porch to her music and having her friends come over and hang out. I even missed her trying to dress us up like little dolls. I never realized how much I would miss my big sister. Not that I wanted her back, mind you. It didn't take me long to figure out that there were certain advantages to her absence. When my parents would leave us alone, I'd be the one in charge, not Barbara, and Christine would have to listen to me. I was just getting used to my new sense of power as eldest child when life threw me a curveball in that regard.

When Barbara married Harry, he had been drafted for Vietnam. He was A1 and his draft number was four! To avoid the infantry, he wisely joined the Navy, hence their move to Norfolk, Virginia. They moved the week after they were married, and one month later Harry went to sea aboard the USS Francis Marion. Since he was supposed to be gone for three months, Barbara decided to come home and stay with us for "a little while." In short, she got married and moved to Norfolk in June and was back in Rockaway by July! All my best-laid plans went out the window. She moved back in, took back our drawer space, and once again relegated Christine to the crib. It was like she'd never left. I couldn't wait for Harry to get back just to be rid of her.

As if her presence wasn't enough of an insult to my new status, she announced she was pregnant! Due to her "condition," a new prominence was bestowed upon her, and Christine and I ended up waiting on her hand and foot. Unsurprisingly, she stayed the whole summer.

25

CHANGES

Helen Nolan, Dad, Babs Kitsen, Bill Walker Holding Jackie,
Buddy Nolan, Mom, Mrs. Brady & Mr. Duffy

Although our wonderful years at Hollyhurst Court came to an abrupt end, there had been numerous indicators that things were changing, and it's been my experience that when things start to change, they change rapidly. A particular situation in 1973 was no different and was a harbinger of things to come.

I was eleven years old that summer and even at that tender age, I could sense change in the air. The Kitsens didn't show up that June, and a family named the Harts moved in next door to us with their infant son. They were a young couple and didn't quite fit in, but they were friendly enough.

The summer after that, the Coogans didn't return and another family moved in next to us. As it turns out, they were related to the Harts. The two wives were sisters. They had a seven-year-old daughter, and she was the first of the new breed of children: smart, precocious, spoiled, and incredibly annoying. She had perfect little dresses and outfits, with matching ribbons and bows and barrettes for her hair. She also possessed the latest, hottest toys, and if that weren't enough, her cat delivered a litter of kittens that summer. We were never allowed to have pets growing up and now she not only had one pet, she had eight! Naturally, Chrissy and I hated her on sight. Suddenly, my sister and I were no longer the darlings of our court, and it's safe to say we deeply resented this turn of events. It didn't help matters any when I witnessed her overfed cat attack and eat one of my injured sparrows. I really didn't like that girl.

Over the next few years, one by one, the families with whom we had shared our summers with for so many years, left for greener pastures. I think the Duffys and Fays were the last holdouts along with my family. During the summer of 1974, two lifeguards moved into the Coogans' bungalow next to us. Christine and I may have been the only ones in the court who completely accepted our new neighbors. Their names were Steve and Glenn and they were big, bronzed, gorgeous, and we adored them!

Then there was the young, British, hippy couple that moved into the Brady's bungalow. They were really nice people with a daughter named Suzanne whom we all liked, but they did the strangest thing: they winterized their bungalow! We'd never heard of such a thing. They opened the bathroom wall to enclose the shower stall, installed insulation, drywall, and a heating system, put down shag carpet, and lived there year-round. At the time, I remember my parents commenting that it would be nice to have people living in the court during the other nine months of the year to keep an eye on things. I hadn't realized things needed to be so closely watched, or why.

26

CHILDHOOD VICE

Barbara & Robert

My first nephew, Robert Sylvester Denny, was born in Brooklyn on February 11, 1974. Barbara, Harry, and the newest member of the family returned to Norfolk in March. In June of 1974, Harry shipped out on the USS Coronado for six months and, you guessed it, Barbara and child came to Rockaway for the whole summer. Why wouldn't she? She'd have free room and board, she'd get to hang out with her friends, and most important, she'd have a free, full-time babysitter: me. We couldn't get rid of her.

So Barbara, with her new status as mother, was back among us, and now we had to make room for a baby as well. Our bungalow was getting smaller by the minute. Robert came with all the accoutrements: crib, playpen, bounce seat, toys, and an unending supply of dirty diapers. Our kitchen was overflowing with Similac, Ak-mak, and Gerber's, and by the end of that summer I was addicted to pureed baby food. You'd never have guessed Barbara was a new mother that summer. She took up with her friends as though she'd never left and with a couple of grandparents to keep an eye on things and two siblings she could boss around at will, it seemed her lifestyle hadn't changed a bit despite her new designation as wife and mother. Chrissy and I were like a couple of little servants. We fed Robert, changed him, walked him, bounced him, watched him, played with him, and took care of him in every way. Our bungalow life revolved around his sleeping patterns and to this day, I resent having to tiptoe around sleeping babies. With all this newfound responsibility on my twelve-year-old shoulders, it's really no wonder Chrissy and I broke loose whenever we could and found ourselves up to our necks in mischief.

When I look at children today and the wholesome lives they lead, I cringe at the things we got into in our youth. Maybe kids grew up faster then. Maybe it was because we grew up in NYC. Maybe we weren't as bad as I think. The summer wasn't as structured as the other nine months of the year and we were allowed to stay out later at night. We were on our own, pretty much free to do as we pleased, and since there was no particular place to be, we slept in as late as we wanted to in the morning, except on Sundays. We always went to an early Mass so we could have the rest of the day for ourselves. There were no soccer camps or art seminars or play dates. All I know is that we tried just about everything at a fairly young age.

When Christine and I start to reminisce about our childhood, it seems harmless and innocent enough. Then one of us will remember that we were smoking cigarettes at ten or eleven years of age and drinking beer by the time we turned fourteen. We knew these things were taboo, and our parents, well, they didn't exactly sit down and explain addictions, medical problems, or how we would screw up our lives. Instead, they were forever threatening us with bodily harm should they ever catch us doing those things. To us, it was stuff that grownups did and they always seemed to be having fun doing it. Back then, everybody smoked, and drinking was reserved for special occasions when you could relax and enjoy it.

It wasn't just Christine and me. All of the kids with whom we hung out did those things, too. Lest people think we were a bunch of derelicts in the making, let me put things in perspective. Smoking entailed stealing a cigarette from an adult and pocketing a book of matches without being caught. Then you'd round up five or six of your friends and find an out of the way spot, generally four or five blocks from your house. You'd post a lookout and finally light up. Then you'd all share it, taking one puff at a time, being careful not to Bogart it. Oh, yeah: we didn't inhale either. This was something that occurred when the opportunity presented itself, like when your mother was out of the house and left a pack of cigarettes sitting in plain view on the kitchen table. It didn't happen all that often and we'd feel so guilty about it that we'd all end up confessing our dirty deeds in the confessional the following Sunday. We could never be mistaken for chain smokers.

Drinking involved a bit more planning. None of us was into anything more potent than beer, and sneaking a beer out of your house was a lot harder than a cigarette. Besides, you can bet somebody would notice a bottle missing from a six-pack. First, we had to pool our finances. (Sure, everything cost less back then, but our allowances were smaller, too.) Then, if you had enough cash, somebody would have to exchange it for larger bills. You couldn't buy beer with a pocketful of quarters. Then came the tricky part. We'd send the oldest-looking member of our crowd to Allen's Deli where he or she would hang outside and ask an adult going into the store if they would buy the beer for us. This was risky because we knew everybody, and if it got back to our parents, we would all be dead meat. You had to find a stranger, which was actually a hard thing to do. Sometimes we'd get lucky and find an older kid whom we knew and he would take pity on our pathetic selves and buy the beer for us. This would be unheard of today, but it was not back then.

Again, I have to put this into perspective. We couldn't very well walk the streets with a case of beer or even a six-pack in a bag. Anybody who saw us would know what it was. And what if we ran into one of our parents? I can see it now, walking along Rockaway Beach Boulevard and running into The Scope (our nickname for my mom). "Whatcha got in the bag, Jimmy?" she'd inquire. He'd smile and say, "Nothing, Mrs. Farish. How you doin'?" "Nothing, my ass," she'd reply as she took the bag out of his arms with one hand and grabbed me by the hair with the other. No, we had to be sneakier than that. So, we'd buy a quart bottle of beer and one of us would hide it under a sweatshirt or in a jacket. Then we'd go three or four blocks out of our way and sneak up to and under the boardwalk. Eight or ten of us would sit under there in the dark and share a quart bottle of Colt 45, making sure not to Bogart it. After three or four sips we'd think we were drunk and having the time of our lives. Afterward, it took even more of an effort to make sure we didn't go home with beer breath. Truth be told, it was more trouble than it was worth.

In due course, as we got older, we began buying packs of cigarettes and cases of beer, but that wasn't until we were sixteen or seventeen. Once more, the whole gang would share the pack of cigarettes and a case of six ounce "nips." I don't remember anybody ever getting into hard liquor, but in our late teenage years, we did experiment with marijuana. My own personal experience with pot consisted of taking a couple of drags off a joint, getting very fuzzy-headed and throwing up in the bushes. That was the extent of my drug encounter. Some of the other kids got into it a little more, but since it was expensive, it never became a regular occurrence. However one particular incident is worth mentioning.

Christine was always up for making a quick buck and over the years she'd come up with various schemes. I don't remember how it happened, but she came into possession of a dime bag of pot. Maybe she found it, maybe she stole it, who knows. Anyway, she wasn't going to waste the opportunity by smoking the stuff. No, she was going to sell it. Now, for any other kid, the proceeds from the sale of a dime bag would have been enough. Not for Christine. She needed to squeeze as much cash from this cow as she could. So she enhanced her stash with additives. She put in some oregano and other herbs. But that still wasn't enough. She found a weed growing in the flowerbeds up at the boardwalk that had a marijuana-like smell. So she ground it up and mixed it in. She cut in so much stuff that her dime bag became three dime bags. She rolled as many joints as she could and proceeded to sell the stuff to our friends. Soon she had a reputation as the dealer with the best stuff in town. Know why? Every time somebody smoked one of her joints, his eyes would water, his nose would run, and his head would get stuffy, and all the kids thought this was a great high. It's no wonder they had that particular reaction: for Christ's sake, they were smoking pollen. When her supply ran out, she gave some cock-and-bull story about her supplier having to relocate and for weeks all everybody talked about was how they might never again get to smoke such good stuff. It's a good thing none of them had severe allergies.

Without a doubt, though, our biggest vice was being boy crazy. All of our girlfriends were and it was foremost in our minds all summer long. Rosemary was constantly concerned about kissing boys because of her braces. Karen developed faster than the rest of us and she was always complaining about being felt up. Tara couldn't wait to start developing so somebody would try to feel her up. Christine was off in the bushes kissing every boy who came along, and I fell in love with someone new, almost daily.

The summer of 1974, I had a huge crush on Patrick, one of the blond surf gods in the neighborhood. He lived in the court right next to ours and was an integral part of our gang for the few summers he spent in Rockaway. It was a good thing he wasn't around for very long since his good looks caused quite a bit of trouble among the girls. Every single one of us had a crush on him. Not surprisingly, he ended up going out with my sister, Christine, and once they became an item, my whole attitude toward him changed abruptly. Patrick was a natural leader and the kids tended to follow him. So, of course, I felt he was a threat to my position within the group and I became increasingly hostile to him. Our association ended when I went after him one night. We had all bought ice cream from the Mister Softee ® truck and were hanging out in the front of the truck, next to the driver's seat. Patrick was sitting in the driver's seat, but I told him to get out because it was my turn. But he didn't move. Well, all I saw was red. I went ballistic. I dragged him out of the chair into the street and proceeded to pound on him. The fight ended with a trip to the hospital, where he got six stitches in his ankle, thanks to a well-placed kick. Hey, I fight like a girl. My parents took him to the hospital and paid the bill since I was the responsible party. I got the beating of my life and was grounded for the rest of the summer. As if that weren't bad enough, I lost the respect of my friends, and my sister wouldn't speak to me. Looking back, it's obvious I was jealous because he chose Christine instead of me. I'd never acquire a boyfriend at that rate. Besides, what guy wants to hang out with a girl who is tougher than he is? His family didn't return to Rockaway the following summer.

By the mid-1970s, Rockaway's downward slide into oblivion was well underway. Court owners were having trouble getting the prices they wanted for their rentals. Consequently, bungalows stood empty for the whole season. No rent to collect meant no funds available for maintenance and improvements, which in turn caused more bungalows to go tenantless. Nobody wanted to stay in a run-down court.

Being the mischief seekers we were, we created numerous opportunities for adventure with these abandoned buildings. At first, we'd find a way to gain entry to one and just poke around. Soon we were using them as clubhouses. In one small court on our block, each of us took one of the bungalows for our own, so we each had our own clubhouse, and we were always arguing about which one we would hang out in. I had an edge in this because I'm a bit of a neat freak, so my club was always the cleanest.

One afternoon during the summer of 1975, a group of us was hanging out in Cynthia Court. It was completely abandoned by this time and we had the run of it. I, Chrissy, Karen, Chris, Tommy, and Rosemary were hanging out in the courtyard when a photographer approached us. He was taking pictures all over Rockaway Beach, documenting the disappearance of the summer bungalow culture. He asked if he could photograph us hanging out in the court, and we obliged him. It wasn't long before we began showing off, as children are wont to do. Hey, these pictures would make us famous! So, as this guy was snapping away with his camera, Tommy yelled over to him, "Hey, mister, watch this!" and then did a kung fu kick straight through one of the bungalow windows. I think he meant to pull his kick, but the momentum carried his leg all the way through and, boy, did he scream. Blood was everywhere.

The photographer picked Tommy up off the ground and asked, "Where does he live?" I told him I lived right next door and that my mom was home. So, he followed me at a dead run with Tommy in his arms into Hollyhurst while I screamed for my mother. Mom immediately assessed the situation—it was bad, wrapped his leg in a couple of towels, and had somebody in the court drive them to the hospital. I wasn't allowed to go with them but Mom eventually contacted his parents and they met up at Peninsula Hospital. There was a lot of glass in his leg and many stitches involved, but it all turned out okay. Tommy was lucky he had not severed an artery. He appeared a couple of days later showing off his war wounds, but he couldn't go swimming for the rest of that summer. Bummer.

27

THE BOARDWALK

Sis bike riding on the boards

The Rockaway Beach boardwalk was one of the longest on the East Coast, with the beach and ocean on the south side. The north side was devoted to recreation: handball courts, basketball courts, flowerbeds, lawns, and long rows of granite checkerboard tables and benches. There were lifeguard offices and concessions every ten blocks or so, but those were the only structures. It ran the length of Rockaway Beach from Ninth Street to 126th Street. It was a traditional boardwalk, elevated and about forty feet wide, built with two-by-fours in a herringbone pattern, with street lamps, benches, water fountains, and railings on both sides. The boardwalk was the main thoroughfare in town. My family rarely used the car at the beach. If you needed to go someplace, you walked or rode your bike on the boardwalk.

The boardwalk was undeniably the social hub of Rockaway Beach. After all, that's where everybody gathered. You couldn't get where you were going without running into dozens of people you knew. If you were looking for someone, you could go up to the boardwalk and ask around, and if your parents were looking for you, they knew where to find you—or would soon enough, heaven help you. During the day, if your parents were on the beach, you would go up to the "boards" and hang out with your friends. If somebody came to the beach looking for you, he or she would stand on the boards until you were spotted. Most importantly of all, the boardwalk was a place to meet and make new friends. The beach was great, but the boardwalk was the place to be.

At night, the boardwalk took on a life of its own. When I was growing up, every Wednesday night at nine o'clock there was a fireworks show launched from a barge anchored offshore. Everybody—and I mean *everybody*—was up on the boardwalk for that. As children, we would walk up with our parents toting beach chairs and grab a spot with the best view. When we got a little older, we'd leave our folks as soon as we spotted our friends and head down to the beach. If we were early enough, we'd climb up onto the lifeguard towers to watch. But most of the time, the towers were already occupied by the older kids having make-out sessions. I eventually turned into one of those older kids and had many a session in those towers. It was a rite of passage.

There was usually at least one party somewhere on the boardwalk each weekend. Sometimes more than one. Anybody could go to these parties, and everybody knew about them. Sometimes people would hand out flyers, but most parties were advertised by word of mouth.

The younger kids would hear about them from the older kids, who heard about them from an older brother or sister, and so on. Even the cops knew. That was fine because we knew all the cops and they knew all of us, but more importantly, they knew all of our parents. So, we were always respectful and, if we were not quite eighteen, we would hide our beers and cigarettes and wave. A couple of times each night they would drive slowly through the crowd, making sure everything was alright, saying hello to the pretty girls and grabbing a beer or two. Each time they came by, there were different cops in the back seat. Everybody wanted in.

Our parents had their own incredibly effective information grapevine and you can be sure they knew when anything was going down. I think my mother was the number one agent in the parents' spy club. All the kids referred to her as "The Scope." It didn't matter what was going on or where it was going on, eventually, at some point in the evening, my mother could be seen taking her "walk" and scoping out the scene. We knew she was there and she knew we knew she was there, and God forbid we were doing something we shouldn't be, which, of course, we usually were. We had our own early warning system: somebody would spot her and yell "SCOPE!" and we'd hide our beers and cigarettes and wave at her, "Hi, Mrs. Farish!" like everything was cool. The severity of the punishment was based on the shape we were in when we got home.

Each lifeguard shack would host a couple of parties each season, and they always had a huge turnout. The girls would show up because the lifeguards were there, and the guys would show up because the girls were there. They'd have these great big barrels of fruit laden, alcoholic concoctions called "jungle juice." The music was loud, the dancing intense, and the skinny-dipping impromptu. The cops did their drive-by's and the Scope, along with several other parents, would take up positions on the other side of Shorefront Parkway to keep an eye on things. Occasionally, some kid would get out of hand and before anyone knew what was happening, a parent would be dragging him off the boardwalk by his ear (or his hair or his shirt) and administering a beating on the way home. We all had our share of that particular experience.

There were a few bars and restaurants on the other side of Shorefront Parkway and patrons inevitably ended up congregating on the boardwalk, cocktails in hand. These strictly spontaneous gatherings would happen on any night of the week. Some kids would spot them and go to check it out. A couple more kids would come along, and then more would join them, and then somebody else would show up with their turntable, speakers, and records, hooking up the equipment to the electrical wires at the base of the lamppost. And wherever there was music, there was dancing. Imagine spending a hot summer night on the boardwalk with a light fog rolling in off the ocean, surrounded by your friends, doing the shag to the latest hit song and having an ice-cold beer to cool down. And then, at some point, the boy you've had a crush on all summer long asks you to slow dance. Life was good.

Then there was "under the boardwalk." What didn't go on under there? When I was a child, the boardwalk was elevated a good ten feet above the sand. Parents, back then, had a certain amount of decorum. They would take the babies under the boardwalk to change a diaper or take a small child there to get out of a sandy bathing suit. During a heat wave, we would all set up our beach chairs and towels underneath it because it was cooler than being under an umbrella. All the parties we had would eventually end up there, where we tried to hide the things we really shouldn't have been doing in the first place.

Years later, with the beach eroding at an unprecedented pace, the city undertook a massive effort to bring in more sand. At one point, you couldn't sit on the beach because there was no sand. At high tide the water came up all the way underneath the boardwalk, forcing people to set up camp on the grassy areas or on the boards themselves. City engineers built a pipeline through which they pumped in sand from offshore. They ran the pipeline on the beach side of the boardwalk and began pumping the sand underneath it. From then on, the boards were only five feet above the sand. This restricted us quite a bit. We used to have parties and dance under the boardwalk. But now it was strictly for making out and going to the bathroom. As large an area as it was, you would still end up tripping over a couple going at it, while looking for a place to relieve yourself. It was dark under there.

28

THE LOVE BOX

The Love Box used to be in this building. It has since
been removed and a window has replaced it.

My parents had their hands full keeping an eye on us during the summer
of 1974. My friends and I were at the age where we began to exert our
independence. In short, we looked for trouble and found it. We hung
out in a spot the whole neighborhood knew as the Love Box.

The Love Box was located on 101st Street between Rockaway
Beach Boulevard and Rockaway Parkway. It wasn't much, really, just
a deeply recessed, extra wide doorway set at loading dock height on

one side of the red brick cloth factory. It doesn't sound like much, but the children of Rockaway Park experienced many of their seminal moments in life at this hole in the wall. Now that I think about it, from across the street it really did resemble an actual hole in the wall. It was almost directly across the street from Callahan's Court and just a little way up the block from our court, Hollyhurst.

When the factory closed for the day, it was all ours. Our parents didn't mind us hanging out there because they could keep an eye on us. More likely, the whole block was keeping an eye on us. Mrs. Frazier could watch us, quite conveniently, from her front porch and it seems to me that she sat there every night. It was the youngest group of kids that hung out there and quite a few of us were too young to cross the street by ourselves. When you grow up in a large city like New York, crossing the street by yourself is a major milestone in life. I don't think I had permission until I was nine years old. If you hadn't gotten permission, stepping into the street without parental approval was cause for punishment and with good reason.

One night we were all hanging out on our side of the street in front of Hollyhurst, sitting on the hoods and trunks of the parked cars. (Does anybody do that anymore? Probably not, what with all the car alarms these days.) Anyway, there was a kid who lived in Bernstein's, the court next to ours, and he was about seven years old. I can't remember his name and boy, is that ironic, as you'll see. His older brother, whose name was Patrick, I think, was there. The seven-year-old kept deliberately stepping off the curb into the street. We told him to stop it and threatened to tell his mother. Not only did he not stop but he kept pushing it. He'd step a little further into the street between the parked cars each time. Eventually, he made a mad dash past the cars, into the center of the street and wouldn't you know it, a car hit him and threw him into the air. Oh God, it was awful. All of the adults in the courts on our street ran out front the moment they heard the car's screeching brakes and our screams. They got him to the hospital immediately and he spent almost the whole summer there. Unfortunately, the story doesn't end there.

Towards the end of that summer, he returned home from the hospital. Physically, he was alright; he had no bodily damage that hadn't been fixed. But he had a bad case of amnesia. On the first night he was allowed out of the bungalow, we all came out to greet him and were hanging out in the exact same spot we had been at the night of his accident. He didn't remember most of us and being kids, we asked him a million questions about what he did remember. Don't ask me what drove this kid to do it, but he ran out into the street again! None of us saw it coming, none of us could stop him and can you believe it, another car hit him! They took him to the hospital *again*. I don't know what became of the boy because we went back to the city a few weeks later Needless to say, his family never returned to Rockaway. I've always wondered about him and hoped it turned out okay. Hey, maybe the second accident gave him his memory back. I swear, you can't make this stuff up.

So, you see what I mean about crossing the street. Our parents would watch us as we crossed over. When we wanted to cross back, we'd yell across the street to whatever adult was around. If there were no adults in sight, the oldest kids would make sure it was safe, looking up and down the street for cars and yell, "Run! Run!" until we were safely on the other side. I remember feeling quite superior once I was old enough to help the younger kids. I'd take the hands of the littlest ones, hold on tight, and race across the street with them, their feet barely touching the ground.

Once on the other side, at the Love Box, we'd all try to squeeze into the doorway. Two people could sit in the back and maybe three could sit on the edge with their legs dangling over the side. Everybody else would have to sit on the cars, so it was important to get there early. The Love Box was our meeting place and clubhouse. We'd draw our hopscotch grids and jump rope in front of it, and for our other games it became either the "jail" or "safety." The kids in the neighborhood naturally gravitated to the Love Box and we all spent many, many hours in it. It was great because it was so centrally located. All you had to do was look across the street to see who was there and what was going on. When we were playing a particularly loud and rambunctious game, the noise would draw other kids out to play with us. Sometimes older kids would come by and evict us or worse, a rival gang would show up and make trouble.

There was one group of kids that usually hung out around the corner on 100th Street. That group included Billy, Peggy, Jacklyn, Michael, and another girl named Karen. My parents didn't care for them and considered them "white trash." We just thought they were tough and were a little afraid of them. Okay, a lot afraid. Our first interaction started with a fight. It was our Karen against Peggy. Karen was big for her age, but Peggy was tough. She looked like a female James Dean. She always had a cigarette hanging out of the side of her mouth and didn't care who saw her smoking. No wonder we were scared of her. Apparently, Karen and Peggy had words one day on the boardwalk and they set a time to fight that night at the Love Box. Word spread quickly enough and quite a crowd showed up for the bout. Our friends got there first and were pumping up Karen to beat the crap out of Peggy, but the moment we saw Peggy and her gang coming down the street, Karen quickly deflated. She was scared and you could see it. Peggy stepped forward while her friends stayed behind her and Karen stepped up and we stood behind her. Starting a fight is a tremendously awkward situation. They tried to stare each other down and talked a bunch of trash while the rest of us stood around shifting from foot to foot, waiting for something to happen. "Yeah, well, your mother wears combat boots." That sort of thing until, eventually, they got down to it. We had been giving Karen tips on how to fight, you know, punch her in the face or in the stomach. To our surprise and Karen's horror, Peggy fought like a girl. She grabbed Karen's hair, spun her around, and flung her to the ground. Peggy jumped on Karen and started slapping her and then got up and started kicking her!

Within moments, Karen was in tears, the fight was over, and Peggy had won. Afterwards, when Peggy and her gang had left, we patted Karen on the back and told her it wasn't a fair fight because Peggy had fought like a girl and yeah, a couple of Karen's punches had landed and she had looked good out there. The fight did nothing to alleviate our fears, so we did our best to avoid those kids.

Unfortunately, later that summer I had a run-in with Peggy. I don't recall what started it but we also arranged to fight at the Love Box. It was the same scene as before: my friends trying to bolster me and then Peggy and the rest of them coming down the block. Only this time, I didn't wait to get started. Before Peggy could get to her spot and make her stand, I was on my feet running at her. I charged her with a body slam and sent her down. She quickly got up and we had a knock-down, drag-out fight punching, kicking, scratching, and hair pulling. I think she had me in a headlock and I had her by the hair when somebody called it a tie. After that episode, we were no longer afraid of them and by the end of the summer, we all hung out together occasionally.

I don't know exactly how the Love Box got its name, but my guess is it had something to do with all the kissing that went on in there. Being in the shadows, it was a natural spot for romance. Right next to the Box on the side of the building, someone, years and years ago, had spray painted MIKE LOVES DONNA. Romances too numerous to count blossomed in the Love Box. Tommy and I had our first kiss there. Christine kissed Chris in the bushes for the first time, but I caught them in the Box on numerous occasions. Rosemary, Karen, Tara, Maureen, and Barbara all experienced puppy love's first rush in that darkened doorway in much the same manner as all the generations that went before us. It's no wonder our parents were keeping a close eye on us.

THE ROCKAWAY CHRONICLES

Dad & Chrissy

Farish Family—Barbara, Paul, Jackie, Dad, Chrissy, Mom

Nephews Harry & Robert Denny

Harry & Jackie

Jackie & Mom on Pat's boat

Jackie dressed for Sunday Mass

Jackie -Hobo Parade

Jackie, Chrissy & Pat Vitale

JB & Jackie at Breezy Point

Matty Coogan—Hobo Parade

Mom & Chrissy

Mom & Dad

Mom & Gertie Toomey

Mom—Hollyhurst Court costume party

Peggy McShea & Mom

Mom & Jackie on Ferry

Jackie holding Jesse & Chrissy in Breezy Point

Pool Party: Paul, Barbara, Cousins, Bill, Lorraine, Fran & Ray

Pool Party: Cousins Fran & Jackie, Uncle Tony,
Aunt Isabel, Jackie, Uncle Micky

Pool Party: Cousins Ray, Fran, Jackie, Nephew Jessie, Aunt Jo,
Uncle Micky, Jackie, Chrissy, Cousin Peggy, Barbara,
Aunt Isabel, Uncle Tony, Paul, & a very tired cousin Bill

John Balestra & his red Radio Flyer™ Wagon in Breezy Point

Aunt Ruthie, Ann Devaney & Dad

Jackie & Barbara Jean Brady

Barbara & Germaine Coogan

Hollyhurst Court costume party:
Karen Holzwarth & Chrissy

Aunt Ruthie and Uncle Ed

Mom, Peggy McShea, Uncle Tony Farish &
Jeannette Schmidt

29

SEVENTIES SLIDE

The Rockaway Peninsula—Photo Credit: Lawrence Miller

It became glaringly obvious during the mid-seventies that Rockaway Beach was no longer the charming, beachside resort it once was. Rockaway's reputation as a family-oriented, seaside idyll had been tarnished in part by the excessive number of drinking establishments that made it so popular during the prior decades. Alcohol had always been a major part of summer life—did I mention the peninsula was crawling with Irishmen? At one time, Rockaway Beach claimed the distinction of having the highest per capita consumption of Budweiser™ beer. It was no longer referred to as the Irish Riviera except in the most sarcastic undertones. Now, the drug culture had found its way to our shores.

When families began shying away from Rockaway because of crime, rampant alcoholism, or the general decay of the area, the bungalow landlords began renting to anyone willing to pay the price. Vietnam had ended and young adults were in the midst of turning on, tuning in, dropping out, and discovering alternative lifestyles. All of a sudden, there were groups of young people—sometimes five, six, or more—sharing a bungalow for the summer. I remember the first hippies moving into the neighborhood.

No doubt about it, my parents were old-school and they simply couldn't fathom these long-haired, unemployed miscreants who were living communally and, might I add, in sin. They were a different breed from my sister Barbara and her friends. They didn't use any of the usual forms of address for older people. Instead, they called everybody "man." There was no more, "Excuse me, sir." Now it was "Hey, man." I had the distinct impression the older generation didn't care for them at all.

It should come as no surprise my friends and I thought they were terrific. We'd go for rides in their beat-up vans and hang out in their bungalows papered in Jimi Hendricks posters and strewn with beer cans and bongs.

30

DA GUMBA

Godfather Pat Vitale

We always referred to my godfather, Pat Vitale, as "da Gumba," which is Sicilian slang for "the Godfather." He'd been a great friend to my parents since their childhood, and he was always there for my sisters and I until his death. We called him Pat for as long as I can remember, but his given name was Pasqual. His parents came over on the boat from Italy and, as so many children of immigrant parents did back then, changed his name thinking that "Patrick" wasn't as ethnic as "Pasqual" and thus might make life a little easier for him. I guess he wasn't aware of the terrible prejudice the Irish had to face back in those days.

Pat never married and never had any children of his own. We were his family, and he was as much a part of our family as any of us. If a family could have a second father, he was ours. We never went any place without Pat, and he shared every holiday and family event with us. Pat was present for all of our christenings, confirmations, communions, birthdays, graduations, and weddings. He was there for my father's funeral and at the birth of each of my parents' grandkids. He went on every vacation with us: Florida, the Poconos, upstate New York, and Las Vegas with my parents. Pat spent more time in Rockaway with us than anybody else, and I've got the photographs to prove it. He came to California to visit me a few times, visited Christine in Florida regularly, and he saw Barbara and her boys often in the city. My husband and I spent the 2001 holiday season in New York and when my family went out to dinner on Christmas Day, Pat was with us. When I say he was always with us, I'm not exaggerating.

Pat visited us at the beach more than anyone else. He had a few different boats when I was a kid and we spent lots of time aboard them, but I remember one in particular. It was a twenty-three-foot Ski Craft cruiser with a lap strake wood hull. It had a 250 horsepower Mercury inboard motor, a head in the bow, and two sleeping berths. Pat had all the paraphernalia, such as the captain's hat he would let us wear, with the ever-present, puffy orange life preservers. He never named that boat, but he had a brass Chinese character mounted on the side and told me it was the symbol for "double happiness."

Pat kept the boat moored in Jamaica Bay at Rosie's Dock, which was located about 88th Street in Rockaway on the bay side. Pat loved expensive toys of all kinds: cars, boats, cameras, etc. He was in charge of the motor pool at the Brooklyn Armory during his many years in the

Army Reserves, so he was pretty good with mechanical stuff. As much as he loved his boats, however, he finally concluded that he wasn't cut out for a seafaring life. He sold his last boat sometime during the late '60s because, as he once told me, he was "a hazard to himself and anybody or anything that got near his boat."

During the years he had boats, Pat took family and friends out for plenty of day cruises. He and my Uncle Mickey were big water skiers and I understand they even got my mother to try it a couple of times. During the summer, he would take their gang for day trips all over the Jersey Shore, the eastern tip of Long Island and Barnegat Bay, and around to Block Island. Sometimes we'd stay in Jamaica Bay, and other times we'd go around Rockaway Point into the ocean.

Regrettably, Pat was never any good with directions and couldn't read a map to save his life. Since he wasn't proficient at navigation, when he was on the boat he would judge distances based on the size and location of the Empire State Building, which during the late 1960s was still the highest building in the world. If he was headed out to Keansburg, and the Empire State Building was only an inch tall between his thumb and forefinger, he'd gone too far. We all witnessed him do this, I swear, and everyone liked to think he was only kidding around. But it was his major reference point and how he navigated all those years.

Of course, without an understanding of marine maps, Pat inevitably ended up stranded on sandbars. Or worse. One night, he was on the boat with his then girlfriend, Dottie Eustace, to watch fireworks off Long Island. It was a dark, moonless night and he couldn't see anything except the lights from the airport. He was focused on the lights and ran the boat onto an island. That rocky night was the end of that relationship.

Another time he was returning from visiting the McDonald family in Barnegat Bay. One of the McDonald kids, an older daughter, was looking for a ride into the city and asked Pat if he could take her back with him on the boat. As they were leaving the bay, she noted the flags the harbor patrol was flying and mentioned the storm warning to Pat. They decided to head out anyway. It was the fastest ride to the city she'd ever gotten: The return trip took half the usual time because they rode a series of huge waves all the way into New York harbor.

Pat was never good with driving directions either. We never made it to any destination without getting lost and one time even ended up in jail. Or I should say, he and my Dad ended up in jail while my mother, Christine, and I sat in the police station lobby. Pat was driving us to Uncle Ed's house in upstate New York and we were pulled over by a state trooper for what we thought was a minor driving infraction. As it turns out, Pat's license was expired, the car registration was expired, and he had no insurance. When Dad tried to slip the trooper some cash, he took us to the police station and had Pat's car impounded. Uncle Ed came to bail them out and we were lucky enough to be able to go to court the same day to take care of the matter. Maybe "lucky" isn't the right word. Uncle Ed, who was somewhat acquainted with the judge, made the comment, "It's too bad we had to meet like this, instead of over a ham sandwich." It turns out the judge was Jewish and took offense at the statement. He refused to release Pat's car and we piled into Uncle Ed's car for the uncomfortable drive to his house, with my mother shooting daggers at the three of them.

31

SUMMER JOBS

Playland—Photo credit: Lawrence Miller

Once we were old enough to work—you could get your working papers at thirteen—all of my friends found summer employment. Rockaway was a great place to get a summer job and there were many from which to choose. With an amusement park, arcade games in the Midway, and food concessions to spend our hard-earned dollars on, we were desperate for a little extra cash. I worked at various jobs each summer and didn't think anything of bouncing from one to another.

My first job, when I was thirteen, was at Martin's Corner. MARTIN'S CORNER—OPEN 24 HOURS. Yes, it certainly was. Initially, I worked at the hot dog counter. I took the orders and worked the register. One hot dog was a "single," two was a "double," three was a "triple," and, you guessed it, four was a "homerun." I'd yell back to the kitchen and in short order the food would materialize under the hot lamps. It was fun for a while because it was so centrally located on Rockaway Beach Boulevard, across the street from Playland, and all of my friends would come by at some point each day. The mornings would be busy because everyone came by for coffee and doughnuts. Martin's had the best. I was a good little worker and moved rapidly up the concession ladder. I was organized, kept a clean counter, and most importantly, my register never came up short. I got the impression a lot of summer employees had light fingers. Eventually, I was placed at the front counter and was given the opportunity to work the busier shifts on which I could make more in tips. This trajectory came to a screeching halt, however, the day I discovered bugs in the pizza cheese containers. I advised the manager of the situation and told him I'd need some help cleaning them out. Well, he wasn't about to waste perfectly good cheese because of a few bugs. UGH! I informed him that I couldn't work under those conditions and gave my notice. He didn't seem to mind and paid me for my work that week. I never ate at Martin's again. So much for my career in the food service industry.

Luckily, I landed a job almost immediately across the street in Playland at the ice cream stand. That was a good job because as an employee, I could go on the rides for free. I learned all the secrets of the Fun House and Haunted House and grabbed bucketfuls of the brass rings on the carousel. The following summer I worked at the cotton candy stand and I quickly learned you *can* eat too much cotton candy.

We all put in time as junior lifeguards. These weren't actual jobs and we didn't get paid, but who cared about being paid because we got to hang out with the lifeguards! They gave us minimal training—hand signals and whistle blows—and told us to keep our eyes open. We were all great swimmers. We wore orange t-shirts and whistles around our neck and occasionally got to hang out in the tower. We never performed any rescues; we could assist after the rescue was performed. But being a junior lifeguard was cool, and it was a way to keep abreast of the parties and events around town. Lifeguards were always at the center of the social hub and we insinuated ourselves as best we could.

One summer I worked at the dart game concession, which was located across the street from Playland. A couple named Marian and Morris owned and operated it. These people were real carnies. They worked for only three months each summer and made so much money they didn't have to work the rest of the year. That's how good they were. I always thought the idea of the games was to win prizes. Hah! That's what the unsuspecting people who play them think! I know better. God, the things I learned working there. First off, they hired me because I was pretty. They wanted to attract boys because boys are traditionally the biggest spenders. They were very up front about this and I was cool with it. Hey, I wanted to attract boys, too. Then they started showing me the little tricks to prevent people from winning. I had a hard time comprehending this. Didn't you want people to win so they'd be happy and come back? Apparently not. I was shown exactly how much air to put in the balloons. Under-inflated balloons don't pop as easily as full ones. If a dart hit the Lucky Strike, it had to be fully within the red circle to count and not on the letters. When people were throwing darts, I was supposed to stand as close to them as possible and yell repeatedly, "Player throwing, here we go, player throwing!" This was supposed to distract them.

Once or twice every summer, the ringers would come by and you can bet that Marian and Morris knew every one of them. When they picked up the darts, we pulled out all the stops. Morris, who had Parkinson's Disease, did and said everything twice. You can imagine how annoying that was. He'd stand there and shout at the top of his lungs, doing double takes all the while and Marian would slam the hinged, wooden counter, which made the whole ledge shake and I was supposed to wave my arms as much as possible. The object was to prevent some poor schmuck from winning his girlfriend a stuffed animal and it almost always worked. Almost. I was secretly overjoyed when a contestant was able to tune out the ruckus and take home the giant stuffed teddy bear. I worked there for two summers before realizing I just didn't have the stomach for it. I really enjoyed watching people win and finally concluded I wasn't cut out for that business.

Then there were the summers I worked on the Mister Softee® ice cream truck. But that story is worth a chapter of its own.

32

BEACH DAD

Mrs. Walker & Tinkerbell in front of the
Duffy's bungalow featuring Dad's sign

I went to sleep away camp for a month during the summer of 1971. It was the first time I'd ever been away from my family for any extended amount of time. I remember my parents giving me a final hug and kiss before I boarded the train at Penn Station along with the other girls headed to Camp Ohneta. I couldn't wait to get there, but once I arrived, I tried everything I could think of to get back home. I was overwhelmingly homesick. I wouldn't eat the food, I wouldn't swim in the lake, and I even tried running away. I was quite the little drama queen.

Eventually, my time at camp ended and my mother was there to meet me when I stepped off the train at Penn Station. As we drove out to Rockaway, I told her how much fun I'd had, but I was more interested in what I'd missed at the beach. I wanted everyone to have missed me desperately and hoped that my friends didn't have too much fun while I was away. She told me I hadn't missed anything, that everything was the same. I couldn't wait to get home.

The entire court was on hand to greet me and welcome me home, and it seemed to me they really had missed me. I felt all grown up, telling my family and neighbors about my adventures. Christine was a little jealous of all the attention coming my way, and naturally, she had to outdo me. She blurted, "Daddy got shot!" My mother called her a bigmouth, but it was too late. I looked at my mother and asked what she was talking about. When she didn't answer me and walked into her bedroom, my stomach did a little flip. She returned and handed me a newspaper clipping and told me to read it. Apparently, my father was entering the subway after work when he was caught in the crossfire between the police and a suspect they were chasing. I read the article, noticed it was dated two weeks earlier and turned my fury on my mother. "My God, Daddy was shot and nobody even called to tell me!" I screamed. I was a member of this family and I deserved to know what was going on! Did they completely forget about me while I was gone? It didn't matter to me that no one considered it a serious injury. The bullet hit him in the meaty part of his upper arm and he was fine. Later that day he showed me the scar. My mother told me they didn't call because they didn't want me to worry. I was just pissed because something newsworthy had happened and I'd missed it. I never went to camp again.

With six weeks of vacation each year, Dad had plenty of time to enjoy the beach, and when my mother was working, he would take us to the beach himself. He was careful not to let us out of the house before slathering us with his own tanning concoction of baby oil and iodine. Why spend money on brand name suntan lotions when he could make his own? We were entirely ignorant of the effects of the sun, and our smooth, dark brown bodies were evidence of this. As a matter of fact, right up until I was about sixteen, most people thought I was Puerto Rican. Not only did we all have great tans, the iodine helped to heal our cuts and scrapes quite nicely as well!

Dad should have had a workshop. He was a born tinker and never let anything go to waste. Over the years he would take pieces of this and pieces of that and create various things out of them. He couldn't walk past a trash pile without seeing something in it that could be put to good use. How many times did he embarrass us kids by picking out an old carriage, or bike parts, or a broken beach chair, and carrying it home? I guess that's what comes of growing up during the Depression.

Dad used to take my older sister Barbara foraging throughout the local vacant lots for things of use. When our court flag decorations deteriorated, he took her to the cloth factory across the street to see what scraps they could dig up to replace the old ones. Then, he'd cut the scraps into triangles, staple them onto twine, and string them from bungalow to bungalow. He repeated this task numerous times over the years.

Our family was the first in our court to have an enclosed shower stall. Initially, there was just a shower curtain between the bather and the rest of the world, and whenever the wind blew, everyone in the court could see who was taking a shower and all that entailed. Apparently, Mattie Coogan would sit on his porch whenever Barbara was taking a shower. So, one day, Dad and Barbara went looking for pieces of wood and with what they found, they built a solid four-sided shower stall. Marcel's Court had just been torn down and there were hundreds of screen doors scattered about the debris. Dad brought one of them home, filled in the frame with scrap wood, and used it as the shower door. He painted it to match the bungalow, tacked down shower curtains to line the interior walls, and installed some shelving. It was a great shower: roomy, comfortable, and private. Soon thereafter, the kids in our court would come by—when their parents weren't around—and ask my mother if they could use our shower. In short order, everyone wanted to use our shower and eventually Dad built one for each house in the court. The neighbors wanted to pay him for the work, but he wouldn't hear of it.

When we were little, Dad built go-carts out of wooden crates, carriage wheels, axels and old bike pedals, and we'd race up and down the street imagining we were miniature Mario Andrettis.

He would bring home broken beach chairs and use the fabric to reweave our own worn beach chairs. Our chairs were a psychedelic fantasy come to life. No part of a beach chair went to waste. If he only had a chair frame to work with, he cut the hollow metal frames to a uniform length, hammered one end flat, and drilled a hole through it. These he nailed at the top of each post on the porch for use as flag holders. Every bungalow in our court had at least two of them. He also used this technique with old batons. Nothing went to waste and he liked to share the wealth.

One summer he found a beat up, old bicycle, brought it home, and fixed it up beautifully. He spray-painted it gold and inserted streamers in the handlebars. When he gave it to me, it had training wheels, but those soon came off. That was my first two-wheeler and he taught me how to ride in front of our court with everybody watching. I couldn't have been more thrilled or excited!

Things must have been slow one day at the lumberyard, because Dad came home from work one evening with identical carved wood signs painted with the surname of each family in our court. He proceeded to install hooks in the center of the front beam of each porch and hung the signs. The mail carrier was thrilled with this, since it made his job easier. He talked about it so much that, eventually, many of the other courts on our street followed our lead and had their own signs made.

By far, though, Dad's greatest claim to fame was the shopping cart. I will never forget that thing as long as I live. Every Friday night, my parents would go grocery shopping but being Friday night, they didn't want to move the car and lose their parking space. Buying enough food for a family of five, they couldn't very well carry the groceries home, so Dad decided to build a shopping cart. Why they couldn't just go out and buy one is beyond me. I mean, everybody had one of those fold up, aluminum, two-wheelers. I have no idea what they used for shopping prior to this and I can't imagine they would have borrowed a neighbor's cart. God forbid you broke it.

One day he brought home some scraps of plywood from the lumberyard. He had four perfectly serviceable wheels from an old baby carriage and a hollow, U-shaped, aluminum frame from the back of a beach chair that fit his creation perfectly. Mom and Dad would walk over to Bohak's grocery store with it and chain it outside until they were finished shopping. It was much too large and unwieldy to take into the store and he made sure nobody was going to walk off with that baby.

Over the years, they utilized that cart for every purpose imaginable, and every one of our neighbors required its use at one time or another. We'd use it to drop off and pick up the laundry. We used it as a baby carriage for our dolls. It became home to the numerous injured birds I'd bring home. We'd use it to transport gear for our beach parties. We all made fun of it but, in the long run, it proved its value and my father could be proud of what he created.

He was always making something out of scraps. Most of it was put to good use but once in a rare while, he'd come up with something and hand it off to my mother and as she looked at it, you could tell she was thinking, "What the hell am I supposed to do with this?"

33

BINGO!

Hollyhurst Court costume party, Dad and Joan Byrne

Dad was big on organized activities, and he was the driving force behind most of the festivities at Hollyhurst Court. For many years, he organized Bingo tournaments for the court residents. Thursday nights were for adults, but Tuesday nights were for the kids. It cost one dollar to enter and each card cost ten cents. While it was supposed to be for the court kids, every kid on the block got wind of it and showed up, and Dad never turned anyone away. He would set up tables and chairs down the center of the courtyard and string bare light bulbs from bungalow to bungalow so we could see what we were doing. There were soft drinks and candy and something nutritious for us to munch on. We played ten games and the winner of the first four games won a dollar. The fifth game was a "round robin" where players had to mark off each square around the perimeter of the card to win. The prize was five dollars—big bucks for us back then. The tenth game was a full card and the winner received ten dollars, and would be very popular for the rest of the week.

Dad set up a table at the back of the courtyard where he could stand to oversee the activities, and then he would close the cage door to spin the wheel while all the kids yelled, "SHAKE THOSE BALLS!" There was no shortage of fun in Hollyhurst. Dad was always organizing something—costume parades, Bingo games, go-cart races—and he made everything fun.

34

PHONES

(or, lack thereof)

Barbara

I mentioned the fact that my parents never had a phone installed in our bungalow. Whenever my sisters or I complained about this glaring lack of modern communication with the world beyond Rockaway, my parents claimed that a ringing phone disturbed the relaxing atmosphere of being at the beach. We all understood that reasoning, but that didn't mean we stopped complaining. It wasn't until many years later that I discovered the true motivation behind Mom and Dad's self-imposed lack of telecommunications.

Recently, while conferring with my sister Barbara, I mentioned the phone situation and she set me straight on a few things. She informed me that we were the only family without a phone; every other family in the court had one. And now that I think about it, there was always a phone ringing in somebody's bungalow and everybody in the court could hear it. I didn't know anyone who had an answering machine at that time and if nobody was home to pick up the phone, the whole court had to tolerate the incessant ringing. However, if the phone kept on ringing, whoever was in the court would assume it was an emergency and go into the empty house to answer it and take a message. Did I mention we never locked our doors? If the message was serious, kids would be dispatched to find the absent resident and relay it.

On any given afternoon, Mom would place her chaise lounge in the center of the courtyard where she could catch the sun's rays. This was generally during the late afternoon when she came home from work or the beach to prepare dinner. She'd place whatever she was making either on the stove or in the oven and then lay outside while it cooked and listen to her records. Many of the other court residents would be home at this hour as well, preparing their own meals.

Mom used to get the biggest kick during those times when one of the phones would start ringing. She would grin and say to Barbara, "Watch this." Everybody in the court would go scrambling into their bungalows to see if it was their phone ringing. She wouldn't move a muscle, basking in the sun with a grin on her face and the knowledge it couldn't be our phone ringing because we didn't have one. She was there to relax, and you couldn't relax properly if you had to jump up every five minutes to answer a ringing phone.

Barbara enjoyed rocking on the porch to music and learned soon enough to appreciate the advantages of being incommunicado. She and Mom would have a good chuckle several times each week. Christine and I were deemed too young to fully appreciate the humor of the situation and remained unaware of the inside joke.

Still, we weren't completely cut off from the outside world. My parents gave a very select few friends and family members a neighbor's telephone number. Ideally, we would only receive phone calls in case of an emergency.

However, the overwhelming reason we never had a phone installed can be summed up in two words: unwanted houseguests.

My parents both came from large families and had an extremely large circle of friends and acquaintances, more than a few of whom were not welcome to show up on our doorstep looking to be entertained, fed, and put up for the night. Most of their friends were too polite to show up unannounced, and since they had no way of contacting us, we were able to head off the vast majority of those looking for a place to hang out and unwind. Thank God for good manners.

But I said, most. Once in a while, some "fringe friends" would come to Rockaway for a day at the beach and then show up at the bungalow in the afternoon saying they were in town for the day and just came by to "say hello." Of course, we had to feed and entertain them and sometimes provide a place for them to sleep, but by not having a phone, we were usually able to avoid this situation. The sheer number of people my parents knew made it necessary to carefully choose those with whom they wanted to spend time. After all, we only had the bungalow for three months each year and entertaining could be costly and exhausting, what with all the food and booze people could consume. As my parents loved to point out to us, money didn't grow on trees.

Those people who did make the cut never failed to show up with cases of beer and soda, goodies from the bakery, or cold cuts and Italian bread from the deli. Those guests were given the neighbor's phone number and would call to inform us of their impending arrival. As a child, I was oblivious to this and, not being privy to the telephone situation, assumed those people showed up unannounced. My parents never deigned to inform us of their social calendar, and I remember being very excited when friends came to visit "unexpectedly." Now I know how my mother was always prepared when houseguests showed up. She wasn't psychic! I wish I'd known that as a kid.

35

GOODBYE, HOLLYHURST

Dad, Chrissy, Jackie & Mom

Our biggest adjustment occurred during the winter of 1975, and it was one of the most devastating things to happen to us as a family. One Saturday afternoon, my parents hastily bundled us into the car and said we were going for a drive but without mentioning the destination. They did this all the time and it would become a game along the way to see if we could guess where we were headed based on landmarks. Soon enough we realized we were headed for Rockaway, which was highly unusual. We never went to Rockaway in the winter. Then my mother explained the purpose of this trip. Mr. Murphy had called the day before and told my father that our tiny bungalow, our summer home for more than twenty years, had been broken into and vandalized. He said we should drive out as soon as possible and we did.

If my parents had known how bad it was, I don't think they would have taken us along. This was no standard robbery. It was blatant hatred. Everything in the bungalow was torn, shredded, ripped apart. Tables were broken into splinters, mattresses were sliced open and gutted, lamps were broken, and dressers were emptied and wrecked. Every single dish, plate, cup, and glass was shattered into a million pieces. Our clothes were ripped up and strewn all over, paint was splashed on everything, and my mother's beloved Bakelite record collection was smashed into tiny pieces. Someone had defecated in the middle of the living room.

At the time, I don't know that Chrissy or I understood just how bad it was, but I do now. When speaking with my family about this incident, I notice we use identical language in describing it: horrible, horrendous, horrifying. Nothing was stolen, so it was a purely personal attack. This was clearly a hate crime, and the idea that anyone could hate us that much was beyond my comprehension.

I remember my mother crying that awful day. That's when the gravity of the situation became clear to me, since my mother very rarely cried, at least not in front of us kids. I don't know if they ever filed a police report. I think not. I got the distinct impression from my parents that things had changed too much and not for the better. The good old days had come to a screeching halt. They were gone and there was no going back. We spent a good part of that afternoon picking our way through the wreckage. We found nothing to salvage and went back to the city empty-handed. We never discovered who did this to us or why.

36

SUMMER IN THE CITY

New York City Skyline

The summer of 1976 was the first summer—the only summer—we stayed in the city. We bought season passes to the community swimming pool on Twenty-Third Street and spent a big part of each day cooling off there with all the other city kids who didn't know the beach as we did. That was the bicentennial year, and all summer long celebrations were held throughout the city. I remember going to see all the boats and ships on the East River and the now famous Fourth of July fireworks display. We took a few trips to the Poconos and upstate New York to escape the heat, but we never headed to the beach. It was a new and different experience for us, but it wasn't Rockaway.

37

CHRISTINE

Little Sister Chrissy

My sister, Christine. Hmmm, where do I start? She's eighteen months younger than I am. You'd think being so close in age that we'd be best friends and inseparable. But it didn't exactly work out that way. We always were, and still are, polar opposites. She was the baby of the family and the only one of us to inherit my father's ice blue eyes. Oh, yes, let's not forget: she was a really, really cute kid who turned into a beautiful young woman—a young woman beautiful enough to start modeling professionally at the tender age of eleven. Let's just say she had a mischievous streak and got away with almost everything. If she had different parents, meaning ones who didn't keep her in check . . . well, I'd rather not go there.

I think maybe she was coddled and fussed over too much as a child. Everything she did was oh-so-adorable and everyone praised her. I don't think she understood the word "no" and when she finally encountered it, she was unable, or more likely, unwilling, to comprehend it. I've always known I could be stubborn at times, but she's taken stubbornness to new heights. Christine was going to do what she wanted to do, and nobody was going to stop her, including, or I should say, especially, our parents. Our parents had their hands full with her and by the time she was a teenager, their only goal in life was to get her through high school. She refused to follow my parents' rules, and they told her if she couldn't obey them, she could move out. By the time she was sixteen, they were at their wits end. Sometime during her senior year, she moved in with her boyfriend, Tracy. She graduated from high school, albeit with four years of summer school under her belt.

Until very recently, Christine has lived life in the fast lane. She wanted to do anything that was new, dangerous, or prohibited. She was the first in our Rockaway gang to try smoking and drinking and drugs. She could curse like a sailor and would shoplift whenever she wanted something she couldn't afford. She disobeyed our parents, disregarded curfew, and held nothing sacred. She was hell on wheels, always in some sort of trouble.

Since Christine had to go to summer school every year, her curfew was earlier than mine. Countless nights I would arrive home on time only to have my mother tell me to go back out, find my sister, and bring her home. I hated doing that. I generally knew where to find her, but she never listened to me. She made me look like an idiot. On the rare occasions when she did get home on time, she always found a way to sneak out again. I'll never forget the night I arrived home to find my parents in a state of shock over the discovery of a window screen that was neatly cut from the frame on one side and the bottom so she could slip out of our bedroom undetected. They simply couldn't fathom this daughter of theirs and why no amount of punishment or threats seemed to faze her. There wasn't much more they could do and when she eventually left the nest, I think they were somewhat relieved but still very much afraid for her.

38

JONES BEACH AND THE SCHAEFER TENT

Jones Beach Theater—Photo Credit: Wikimedia Commons

Once we were in Rockaway for the summer, we very rarely left the beach, but there were always one or two special outings each year. We'd leave Rockaway to go to Palisades Park for a day or out to Long Island for a family event. Nearly every summer, my parents took us to Jones Beach for a night at the theater, and that was a tremendous treat.

Jones Beach is located in Wantagh, NY, out on Long Island. There was a wonderful beach, an amphitheater for concerts, and an outdoor theatre. The stage itself sat on the water with a moat between it and the audience seating. My mother has always been, and continues to be, a huge theater fan and did her best to pass down that love to her daughters.

She loved all types of shows but thought it best to introduce us to musicals at an early age, thinking it would appeal to us the most.

So once or twice each summer, my parents would pack us up in the car and make the drive out to Jones Beach. The shows we saw were always musicals: *Shenandoah, Annie Get Your Gun, Seven Brides for Seven Brothers, Brigadoon,* and *South Pacific.* We'd sit there on the shoreline, bundled up against the breeze, and watch in fascination. As good as the shows were, the best part of the evening came later. After the show, we walked over to a huge red and white striped tent called the Jones Beach Schaefer Tent. Schaefer Beer was the sponsor, hence the name. There was a large orchestra and a good size parquet dance floor surrounded by round, white cloth covered tables. We'd find a table to sit at, generally sharing it with other people, and my father would buy a pitcher of Schaefer for himself and Mom and get us girls some Shirley Temples. Then the music would start. It was the soundtrack of my childhood, with all the big band classics. We'd sit listening to it for a while, tapping our feet and humming the tunes, and then my parents would get up to dance. Boy, could they dance.

I loved watching them. They'd been dancing together for decades at that point and made it seem so effortless. My sisters and I would sit there and watch them Foxtrot back and forth across the dance floor as we made the inevitable comparisons to the other dancers. Not surprisingly, we always thought Mom and Dad were the best out there. I wanted to be able to dance like that and, after working myself up to it, I would eventually ask my father to dance with me. When I was little, he would have me stand on his feet and hold on while he took us around the dance floor. I was staying up late, drinking Shirley Temples and dancing under the stars to an orchestra. I felt like such a grown-up!

I remember very clearly one of those trips to Jones Beach. I was about fourteen years old at the time and we went to see *Annie Get Your Gun*. It was myself, Mom and Dad, and Christine. Barbara was already married and off living her new life with her new husband and baby. We went to the Schaefer Tent after the show and Chrissy and I watched my parents do their thing on the dance floor. I worked up the nerve to ask Dad to dance with me but had no intention of standing on his feet. I was a little too grown up for that now. When they sat down, I made my request and Dad obliged. We got out there and I tried to mimic the steps as best I could but it was hopeless. I repeatedly stepped on his toes and was either bumping into him or pulling away from him. Dad put up a valiant front for my sake, while I was completely embarrassed. The song ended and as he walked me off the dance floor, he whispered to me, "Jac, you've got two left feet—but don't worry about it. We can work on that." So, while I was temporarily mortified, I had something to look forward to. Before we left to go back to Rockaway that night, I was already envisioning myself the following summer, dancing under the great red and white striped tent—elegant, fluid, graceful, that would be me.

39

THE WONDER YEARS?

Chrissy & Jackie

One summer spent in the city was more than enough. It gave all of us the opportunity to understand and cope with the changes. The summer of 1977, my parents rented a bungalow in a court on 99th Street, right across the street from the beach.

I remember the first time we went to check out the new place. I was prepared to hate it. Yes, it was different, and no, we didn't know the other families in this particular court. Maybe this wasn't great timing, considering both Christine and I were navigating puberty while my mother was negotiating menopause. I think we were all prepared to hate it because it wouldn't be the same, but our change of address was just the beginning.

Christine and I were at the crossroads that all parents dread: We were TEENAGERS. Naturally, we rebelled at every opportunity and exerted our independence in every conceivable way. We tried anything and got caught doing everything. We were drinking beer and smoking cigarettes on a regular basis. We stayed out later and later at night, pushing the envelope on curfews. We fell in with some of the more nefarious characters in the neighborhood. Boys took on a previously unheard of significance in our daily existence, and we didn't have any trouble attracting them. That summer, some of the older kids we knew had driver's licenses and suddenly, we were riding around in cars. Oh, we were every parent's nightmare come to life.

Barbara was at a fork in the road, as well. In 1978, she and Harry separated. Her boys weren't yet in school, and she had a rough few years as a single mom. She dated a couple of men, and then she met Paul, whom she married in 1982.

40

WEEKEND PARKING

Jackie waiting to move cars

Many of the families that summered in the Rockaways owned a car and parking wasn't a problem, as there was plenty of street parking and a number of vacant lots. During the weekends and holidays, however, Rockaway would be inundated with day-trippers out for a day at the beach and a night at Playland, so parking spaces were at a premium. This called on the precision planning for which our court was famous.

The night before the masses were to descend upon us, somebody in the court went out to the street to check on the parking situation, and then would go house to house to find out if anyone was expecting guests and how many spaces we needed to "save." The men of our court would jockey their cars into position and park one behind the other. They'd take up just enough space so that a strange car couldn't squeeze in and the next day, when court company arrived, the cars could be pulled forward or backed up just enough to let the arrivals park. You never knew what time company would show up, so the parking maneuvers were a full court effort. When they arrived, they would double park out front—they knew the drill—and after greeting everyone and trying not to seem too anxious, would find out whose cars were to be moved and proceed with the plan. Most of the time, half the court population was already at the beach when guests arrived, so everybody helped themselves to each other's car keys to facilitate the process. It was a testament to life with unlocked doors.

We used this same arrangement whenever someone unexpectedly needed to use his car during peak parking periods. Keep in mind, this could go on for three or four days at a time. If someone was going to the market, she'd check to see if anybody else in the court needed anything. Without fail, half the bungalows needed fresh milk and, if the number of guests was underestimated, an extra case or two of beer. While the shopper was making the rounds, the others sat in their idling cars ready to move into position to save the spot. It was the least we could do. Our parking maneuvers became legendary and were a thing to behold. Naturally, many of the other courts tried to replicate these drills, but they never pulled it off with our finesse.

41

MISTER SOFTEE™

Mister Softee™ Truck

In the spring of 1978, I turned sixteen: the magical, mythical age about which young girls dream. I had just completed my sophomore year of high school and was looking forward to an exciting summer with my friends going to parties and flirting with cute guys.

Once we arrived in Rockaway, I immediately set out to secure a job for the season, as I envisioned a hectic social calendar that would require cash and lots of it. I'd been hanging out in clubs and discotheques in Brooklyn for the last year—my fake ID was excellent—and there was a new club on 115th Street that I planned to patronize that summer.

I'd worked at the dart game concession the prior summer with my friend Barbara. Her employers wanted to hire another young girl part time and asked if she could recommend someone responsible. She told them about me, set up a meeting, and I spent the entire summer perfecting my dart game. I was hoping to be rehired for another season because working the dart concession definitely had its advantages. Located next door to the Paddy Wagon, I met lots of cute guys and, since it was in the heart of the midway, I was in the thick of it with friends coming by constantly. It was never boring and I knew everything that was going on in town.

Halfway through the summer, our friend Jimmy came to me with a proposition, and the timing couldn't have been more serendipitous. At the dart concession, I worked only four hours four days a week. I knew I should find other employment with more hours but I wasn't exactly pro-active in that regard. Jimmy worked on the local Mister Softee® truck with Rob.

I had the biggest crush on Rob. He worked behind the sandwich counter at Allen's Deli on the corner of 101st Street when I was a kid, so I'd known him for a while. He had shoulder length black hair, dark, hooded eyes, and straight, white teeth. I was only ten years old and thought he was gorgeous! I'd find any excuse to go to Allen's just to get a glimpse of him and if I was there to order sandwiches, I would stand at the counter surreptitiously watching him. He was friendly and always had a smile for me because he knew I was Barbara Farish's little sister and his older brother Gerard hung out with Barbara. My crush was renewed each summer when I would see him for the first time. Since he was a few years older than I was and ran with a different crowd, he remained a girlhood fantasy. And it certainly didn't stop my roving eye as far as more likely boyfriend candidates were concerned. Everything changed the summer of 1978.

I've never been a big fan of ice cream, but I ate a ton of it that summer. The highlight of my day was when that truck rolled onto our street, about seven o'clock each evening with the jingle playing on the speakers. I was always first in line and since Jimmy knew about my crush, he always made sure that Rob served me. When Jimmy got off work each night and hooked up with us, I bombarded him with questions about Rob. Does he have a girlfriend? Which beach does he surf on? Any chance he'd be up on the boards tonight? You get the picture.

Halfway through the summer, Jimmy was offered a better paying job at a deli and he couldn't continue to work on the Mister Softee truck. Jimmy's ambition was to have his own deli some day, so this was his chance to learn the business. He asked if I would be interested in taking his place on the Mister Softee truck. For whatever reason, I was very surprised that he should ask me and not one of the other boys. Then he said that it was Rob's idea: he had asked about me in particular. I was speechless for a moment and then came the barrage of questions, the most important one being, *Why me?* According to Jimmy, Rob thought I was cute. He thought I was cute! He wanted me to work with him! He thought I was cute! Thus began our long, convoluted relationship.

Rob would pick me up at my house at four each weekday afternoon for the evening rounds and at noon on the weekends. On the weekends, we worked the beach at Riis Park. The weeknight rounds were fun because I knew just about everyone we served. When we drove around town, everybody waved at us. As we drove up each street with the jingle playing on the speakers, we'd watch all the little kids running in our wake yelling for us to stop. Everybody loved Mister Softee and we were very popular.

I was dating a guy named Bruce when I took over Jimmy's job that summer. He was a year-round resident, two years older than I was, and had an incredibly loud car. He was alright, I guess. He would pick me up from the Mister Softee truck at the last stop of the night, which was usually on 109th Street. After we served the last of the ice cream for the evening, we would shut off the music and outer lights, close the service window, and clean up the inside of the truck. If Bruce wasn't there to pick me up, Rob would drive me home. It wasn't long before Rob and I were making out in the back of that darkened truck. Sometimes we were going at it as Bruce drove up! I'd act as if nothing had happened and be on my merry way. Rob had a girlfriend himself that year.

Soon, however, Rob and I were sneaking around together sans the truck. We thought we were a big secret. Little did we know that everyone in town knew about our romance. Tracy used to tease me relentlessly about Rob and I'd pretend not to know what the hell he was talking about. We played that game for years.

At the end of every summer, you'd break up with whomever you were dating since you wouldn't see him until next summer and we were all realistic about the situation. After all, one could go through lots of boyfriends in nine months. So, I broke up with Bruce and would you believe he had the nerve to ask me to "give him something he could remember me by"? Even at sixteen, I knew a bad line when I heard one. What a jerk. Rob and I were never officially "going out" so we just said, "See you next summer." And we did. And the summer after that, and the summer after that. We saw each other occasionally during the winters but were never officially a couple. We always had significant others in our lives, but we never failed to maintain our friendship . . . until he got married. His wife doesn't believe men and women can be platonic friends. I haven't spoken to him in at least a decade.

42

MUSIC

Barbara's 45's

Music has always been and continues to be an integral component of our family life. None of us ever had any type of formal training or played any instrument worth a damn, but we listened to music, danced to it, and sang along to it at the top of our lungs whenever the feeling took hold of us. My father was a decent singer and my mother had a way with a couple of songs. My sisters and I were middling singers, but that never hampered our enthusiasm.

As children, we were exposed to a wide variety of music, due, for the most part, to my parents' advanced age. Dad was born in 1911 and was one month shy of fifty-one years old when I was born. He was fifty-three when Christine was born. Mom was born in 1925, a truly great time for music. Dad had a phenomenal record collection, and it was so extensive that he had to come up with a system to keep them in some sort of order so he could locate a particular record when he wanted it. He numbered the records in order of purchase and used a red marker to write the number on the back, upper left-hand corner of the album cover. He kept an address book, not for addresses but for artists and their various albums. He listed them alphabetically by artist and then album title and placed the album number next to the album name. It was a good system, that is, until somebody put an album back in the wrong place.

Mom had her own record collection. She kept old seventy-eight Bakelite records and, while her collection wasn't as extensive as Dad's, it was pretty damn impressive for its content. She had recordings of Milton Berle, Charlie Barnett, Les Paul and Mary Ford, Al Jolson, Fred Astaire, Gallager & Sheen, Fats Waller, Rudy Vallee, Scott Joplin and other ragtime artists, Xavier Cugat, Arty Shaw, Guy Lombardo, and Freddy Martin.

Music was always playing in our house, both in the city and at the beach, and we grew up listening to an incredible variety of it. We got blues from Robert Johnson, Billy Holiday, and Bessie Smith. We'd swing along with the big bands, including Benny Goodman, Paul Whiteman, Harry James, Glenn Miller, Tommy Dorsey, Duke Ellington, and Count Basie and their respective orchestras. We sang along with Mitch Miller and the Gang. We crooned with Dean Martin, Perry Como, Mel Torme, Tony Bennett, Nat King Cole, Jerry Vale, Frank Sinatra, and Bing Crosby. We knew the complete works of Louis Armstrong, Etta James, Quincy Jones, Dinah Washington, Louis Prima and Keely Smith, Herb Alpert and the Tijuana Brass, and Sergio Mendez and Brazil 66. My father adored the ladies of song, such as Kate Smith, Peggy Lee, Georgia Gibb, Rosemary Clooney, Brenda Lee, Doris Day, and Connie Francis. Did I mention Dinah Washington? Then there were Nina Simone and Patsy Cline, Sarah Vaughan, and let's not forget Miss Ella Fitzgerald. The list goes on and on. Shall I continue?

We had all the Blue Note recordings; we listened to the best of the Verve Years and most of the Mercury Years. We knew jazz. Boy, did we know jazz! We grew up on Columbia's Jazz Masterpiece samplers. We listened to recordings of John Coltrane, Miles Davis, Thelonious Monk, Chick Corea, Stanley Clark, and Stan Getz, among countless others.

Then there were the soundtracks from theater and film: *Porgy and Bess, Shenandoah, The Music Man, The Sound of Music, Chicago, 42nd Street, South Pacific, West Side Story, The King and I*, etcetera, etcetera, etcetera. Get it?

My sister, Barbara, was born in 1954 and had an extensive record collection of her own, and while it was a far cry from what my parents were listening to, it certainly had its merits. In fact, Barbara's contribution to my musical education was as essential as that of my parents. Thanks to her, I know the words to every Beatles' song ever written. I fell in love with Eric Clapton and his guitar. I have more than a passing acquaintance with the girl bands of the '50s. I know the history of Motown and in my car I become the fourth Supreme when one of their songs comes on the radio. I know who Phil Specter is, and I know more than I want to know about Elvis. Barbara gave me Wilson Pickett, Creedence Clearwater Revival, The Doobie Brothers, The

Four Tops, Aretha Franklin, The Beach Boys, The Mamas & The Papas, Marvin Gaye, The Doors, Simon & Garfunkel, Jefferson Airplane, The Byrds, Three Dog Night, Dick Dale, Dusty Springfield, Chuck Berry and Chubby Checker, Badfinger, and The Chipmunks. I know what's an "oldie" and what's a "goodie." I could go on and on here, but I won't. You get the picture.

Every summer, we transported Barbara's portable record player to the bungalow. While we didn't bring Dad's records with us (he wouldn't dream of transporting his albums anywhere), Barbara brought her carrier boxes bulging with forty-fives. Mom kept her seventy-eights at the beach year-round. When Barbara was at the bungalow, she pretty much had control over the music selection. She would sit on the porch in one of the rocking chairs, listening to her records or the radio, rocking back and forth, back and forth. She knew all the words to every song and would sing along to them, and if Christine and/or I were anywhere in the vicinity, she would recruit us to sing backup for her. She always sang lead. To this day, when I hear specific songs, I automatically sing the backup vocals. So the three of us would sit on the porch rocking away and singing along to our hearts' content, oblivious of what the neighbors thought of us and unaware of how often my father had to repaint the worn spots on the porch because of all that rocking.

43

ADVENTURES WITH BILLY

Cross Bay bridge—Photo Credit: Wikimedia Commons

During 1979 and 1980, I dated a guy named Billy from Staten Island. He worked as a bouncer at a discothèque in Bay Ridge, Brooklyn, and that's where we met. He was tall, six-foot-five, with red hair and blue eyes. Can you say "Irish"? He was a sweet guy and we dated for about two years.

Anyway, Billy would drive out to Rockaway to visit me at the beach whenever he wasn't working. He drove a very well used, decades-old Cadillac, dark blue with a white leather interior, bald tires, and no muffler! That monstrosity was always breaking down. The battery would die, the starter wouldn't start, the belts would snap, the radiator sprang leaks, and it would overheat at the drop of a hat. I remember he had three flat tires in one day! I swear, I don't know how he ever got to his destinations. It goes without saying that he was always late, but since I could hear that thing coming from a mile away, I always had plenty of time to get ready.

Billy had a boat he moored in Jamaica Bay on the Broad Channel side. It was an old fiberglass-hulled cruiser and, like his car, something was always breaking down on it. Since I spent the summers in Rockaway and his boat was moored right across the bay in Broad Channel, we used it frequently . . . when it was running, that is.

On the weekends, if the weather cooperated, we'd take friends and family members out on Billy's boat and make a day of it. We'd pack the coolers with food and drinks and head out to Sheepshead Bay. Sometimes we'd stay in Jamaica Bay to water ski or head around to Rockaway Point just to hang out and swim.

When the tide was high, some of the more daring teenagers would dive off the Cross Bay Bridge for fun. One summer, a local Rockaway boy drowned while doing it. It wasn't suicide, just an awful accident. Some say he was drinking, others say a gust of wind came out of nowhere. I heard that he hit one of the concrete pillars, dropped into the water, and never surfaced.

It just so happened that we went out on Billy's boat the weekend after that occurrence. It was Billy and I, Barbara and her boyfriend at the time, Larry, and Christine and Tracy. We had sandwiches and salads from Allen's Deli and a cooler full of beer, and we stayed in the bay to water ski. We took turns trying out the new skis I'd bought Billy for his birthday that year. We were having a rollicking good time. The day was extremely hot, so we anchored the boat and ended up in the water to keep cool.

We were all treading water when Barbara felt something touch her foot. She squealed and began swimming away from whatever it was. Then, Larry felt something. It was then that Christine yelled, "Oh my God! It's Bobby Dennehy!" We'd completely forgotten that his remains had yet to be found, and here we were, swimming in the same body of water! That really freaked us out and we couldn't get into the boat fast enough. We all swam madly to the back of the boat, fully expecting a bloated corpse to pop up at any second. Every time one of us tried to climb up the ladder, somebody would yank him down so he could get out of the water first. We were crawling all over each other screaming and laughing and Christine kept yelling his name, over and over. Then somebody dove underwater and began grabbing our feet and legs. That really drove us over the edge. We were screaming and thrashing around and laughing so hard, it's amazing none of us drowned. It was mass hysteria. Once we were all back on the boat, we couldn't catch our breath from laughing so hard.

The following week, Bobby's bloated, crab-eaten remains washed up at Pier 92.

44

THERE'S A BACK DOOR?

Mom, Chrissy & the unused back door

One night during the summer of 1980, when we lived in the bungalow on 99th Street, a severe summer storm hit the Rockaways. The bungalow, built entirely of wood, always experienced warping in the door and window frames whenever it rained. The morning after the storm, Mom and Chrissy were rushing to make their respective buses. Mom was going to work and Chrissy, about to start her senior year, was going to summer school.

When Chrissy tried to open the front door, it was so badly warped, it wouldn't budge. The two of them worked feverishly to pull the door open, but to no avail. Mom eventually said to Chrissy, "Why don't you go out the back door and run around to the front porch, then you can push, and I can pull the door open?" So, Chrissy ran past Dad in the kitchen, out the back door, around to the front of the house, up the porch steps, butted her shoulder up to the front door and began pushing, with Mom pulling from the inside. Once the door was open, they breathed a sigh of relief, grabbed their bags and ran for the bus.

Dad just stood there watching the whole episode. Why they couldn't have left through the back door was beyond him.

45

MORE (DANGEROUS) ADVENTURES WITH BILLY

Jackie & Billy

Far Rockaway was a predominately black neighborhood and wasn't a particularly safe place to be, especially at night. There were quite a few low-income housing projects complete with gangs, drugs, and high crime rates. This was not an area I nor any of my friends frequented, and our parents and older siblings repeatedly warned us not to go there.

One Saturday night, Billy wasn't working and decided to come cut to Rockaway unannounced with three of his bouncer friends. I was out with my friends at the local disco, spending an inordinate amount of time on the dance floor with a cute guy I had just met. One of my girlfriends came up to me and said Billy had shown up and was looking for me. I spotted him and tried to duck out of there but it was too late. He'd already seen me—dancing with Mr. Cutie. Apparently, he'd gone to the bungalow and Christine had told him where I was. Traitor! Billy and I had a big scene and I told him I was going home. He said he'd drive me, but I refused, and we got into another fight in the parking lot. It ended with me getting into the car with Billy and his friends.

On the way home, driving along Shorefront Parkway, another car drove up alongside us. The four or five guys in the car were looking for trouble. They revved their engine, we revved ours and tore out, burning rubber and hurling insults along the way. I started getting nervous and told Billy to turn around, but his friends were ready to do battle and egged him on. One of them mentioned there was a bat in the trunk. And that's when I felt the first tingle of fear trickle down my spine. Next thing I know, we were driving on side streets in Far Rockaway. We had lost them somehow, and we were driving up and down the darkened streets looking for them. Wouldn't you know it, the damn car stalled! We were five white kids, *really* white kids, stranded in the middle of Far Rockaway at two o'clock in the morning. We got out and pushed the car into a parking space and the guys grabbed whatever they could use as weapons. There was indeed a bat in the trunk, along with a crowbar. One of the guys had a set of "brass knuckles". Nice crew, huh? They also grabbed a flashlight.

I don't know what the plan was: I just knew we had to get the hell out of there. All of a sudden, we heard noise coming up the street and it got louder and louder. Just before we turned the corner we looked back to see a small mob headed our way. It was our guys alright, and they had reinforcements. We started running. So did they. I was so scared, I couldn't think. I was in pure survival mode. We were in a residential section of town and when we couldn't outrun the mob, we tried ducking into alleys and then backyards. At one point we were going from one backyard to another, over fences and walls. Dogs were barking and chasing us, people were yelling at us. It was terrifying.

We found a corner in a backyard where we were able to huddle down and hide for a while. The guys thought the only way to get out of this was to head for the beach and hide under the boardwalk until it was safe to go back to the car. But they were afraid I couldn't keep up with them. They needed to stash me someplace and then make a run for the beach. The next thing I knew, Billy was pounding at the back door of the house we were hiding behind. An elderly, black woman opened the screen door and pointed a shotgun at us. Billy just started talking, telling her there a mob was after us, and begging her to please take "the girl" into her home. I was scared to death! We could hear them coming down the street searching for us. Then the woman grabbed me and dragged me inside. Billy swore they'd come back as soon as they could get the car started, and off they went.

The woman took me into the living room and told me to sit down "in that chair where I can see you.". I couldn't see anything because she didn't bother to turn on the lights. So, I sat down and she sat across the room from me with that shotgun in her lap. We could hear the mob go by the house. I was frozen, like a scared rabbit. I don't know how long we sat there like that. Eventually, she said to me, "Does your Momma know where you are and what you're doin?" I said, "No, Ma'am." That was the extent of our conversation.

Eventually, I heard Billy's car pull up in front. The old woman looked out the window and then peeked out the door and gestured to me. "Go on," she said.

As I squeezed by her in the doorway, I looked her in the eye and said, "Thank you. Thank you. I think you saved my life tonight." She didn't reply.

I ran to the car and got in, and off we went. We drove out of Far Rockaway slowly with the lights off and I think I held my breath until we were safely back in Rockaway. I crawled into my bed at home and my final thought before falling asleep was, "Oh God, if my mother ever finds out what happened tonight..."

Note: My mother learned about this story when she read the first draft of this book. She didn't believe me.

46

ROCKAWAY NIGHTLIFE

Chrissy & Tracy

There was no shortage of nightlife in Rockaway Beach during the '50s and '60s, and Irish Town was notorious for its "One Hundred Bars." There were one hundred drinking establishments within a ten-block stretch from 95th Street to 104th Street, and that's dense by any standard. Try to imagine walking by ten bars on every block. In Rockaway, you didn't have to use your imagination.

A number of these establishments had closed by the '80s, but still quite a few remained. There was Connelley's, Howley's, Hickey's, O'Gara's, The Paddy Wagon, The Irish Circle, Flynn & McLaughlin's,

Dingy Dan's, Brennan's, Fitzgerald's, Healy's, Tuberty's, Mahoney's, and Fitzgerald's. There were actually a few watering holes without Irish names, if you can believe that: The Raintower, Snug Harbor, and Boggiano's. Um, I think that's it. Live entertainment was the key, and many of those places had it covered.

Sometime during the early '70s, Rockaway Beach had the infamous distinction of consuming more Budweiser™ per capita than anywhere else in the country, due, for the most part, to the excessive number of drinking establishments. That was in 1973, and everybody in town wore T-shirts commemorating that stupendous achievement. Oh, we were like a bunch of proud parents: it was all anyone talked about that summer, and you can bet we did everything in our power to ensure we kept the title. Bud *flew* off the store shelves.

O'Gara's was across the street from Playland on Beach 98th Street and it rocked. John O'Gara was the proprietor. It was a cavernous place with a huge square bar, a stage, and a dance floor, and there was live music almost every night. If you were anywhere within a three-block radius of O'Gara's, you could hear the music—even if you were in another bar with its own music.

For a number of years, O'Gara's had a live band that played the oldies and, during the second set, they'd bring out an Elvis impersonator. He was very good and knew how to work a crowd. It was generally standing room only. He sang all the great Elvis hits and would throw his scarf into the dancing throng and all the girls would scream. What a scene it was! It was a family establishment, and children were not only permitted to be there but were encouraged to dance right along with the adults. On any given night, you'd find three or four generations of one family sitting at one of the tables or booths.

All of our friends had curfews, usually eleven o'clock. Many Saturday nights, when Christine and I would get home, we'd find a note from our parents saying they were over at O'Gara's and, well, it seemed like an invitation to us. I mean, what else were we going to do? Stay in the house by ourselves? So, we'd head over and join them. Hey, we had a curfew and this was a way to stay out later. Soon enough, all our friends knew about Elvis and they would get permission from their parents to join us. We were smooth operators and could work a curfew inside out and every which way.

Toward the end of the summer of '79, The Paddy Wagon was our scene of choice. It was right in the heart of town across the street from Playland on Beach 98th Street. When I was growing up, the drinking age in New York was eighteen. Naturally, we all had fake identification by the time we were fifteen or sixteen. Drinking was not the issue it is today. We weren't driving around in cars, we'd never heard of date rape, and the older kids always looked out for the younger ones. Tossing cookies under the boardwalk was generally the worst that would happen. Then your friends would clean you up and get you home. This was during the '60s and '70s and, despite those turbulent times, it all seemed terribly innocent.

I was seventeen during the summer of '79. Being a little older than most of my crew, I was the one to make inroads at the Paddy Wagon. I was working again that summer at the dart game concession, which was located right next door. With a little bit of luck, some charm on my part, and the fact that my older sister was quite popular, I became friendly with a couple of the bouncers working at the Paddy Wagon, Tracy and John. Tracy worked as a lifeguard during the day and John was biding his time waiting to be called up for the fire department.

Another bouncer named P.G. used to date my sister, Barbara. On nights when the bar was slow, they would come over and hang out with me while I worked.

Eventually, I showed up one night after work and they let me in. They never gave me a hard time with my ID and always kept an eye on me to make sure nobody was bothering me. I think it was Liz who first went in with me. She was tall for her age and looked a little older than she was. The Paddy Wagon had live entertainment on the weekends and a great jukebox the rest of the time. It was dark and dirty and loud, exactly what any teenager in her right mind was looking for.

At the Paddy Wagon, I learned how to throw a mean game of darts and how to down a shot without gagging. I danced to the live, loud, awful bands that played there, and I'll never forget the night Tracy and I got up on top of the bar and danced to the cheers of the crowd. I was there the afternoon a friend of ours rode right in off the street on his new Harley and took a few turns around the bar before he came to a stop and ordered a drink. We all crowded around admiring his new wheels and toasting his good fortune. I asked him to take me for a ride on it and he said he would as soon as he bought a second helmet. I badgered him for days about that ride. He died on that bike only two weeks later when he crashed into a column under the El. He never got around to getting that second helmet, and maybe it's a good thing I never got that ride.

Tracy and I became friends and, in due course, I was able to gain entry for the rest of my crew. One night, I took my sister, Christine, with me and Tracy took one look at her and fell head over heels. Chrissy and Tracy were a hot item for many, many years and this was great for all of us because Tracy was a very popular guy and he could get us into every hot spot in town.

Tracy later became hugely successful with his bar, Siberia, located in Manhattan, and was mentioned regularly in the New York newspapers. My mother would send me clippings to keep me up to date on his escapades. John went on to become a New York City firefighter. Just a few years into his career, he was badly injured on the job and could have retired with a full pension. He chose not to and was back on the job in a remarkably short time. A few days after 9/11, I heard from Robert, then a member of the NYFD, that John, a captain, was one of the first to respond to the World Trade Center attack. He and seventy-five other residents of the Rockaway peninsula died that terrible day.

The Irish Circle was another establishment we frequented, located on the corner of 102nd Street and Rockaway Beach Boulevard. It's been there for as long as I can remember and was originally owned and operated by the Woods family, who also had rooms to rent upstairs and in the back. Many of the pubs in Rockaway were strictly drinking establishments, but not The Irish Circle. It was as much a restaurant as it was a bar, and people went there specifically to eat traditional Irish fare. The Irish Circle also specialized in traditional Irish music and over the years booked many of the great Irish bands and musicians from all over the world. The Circle was a terrific example of a business geared toward family. Parents, children, and grandparents would have dinner together and afterward take turns dancing a jig. No one ever minded having children underfoot, and it wasn't unusual to see a mother holding one sleeping child in her arms while another had his head in her lap.

My family went frequently to the Circle, and I always made a point of stopping in whenever I was in town. The Woods family sold it long ago, and it has undergone many reincarnations. At one time, it was a sports bar. Then it went through a karaoke phase. A few years back, the owners tried to restore the Irish pub atmosphere. But by that time, the families were no longer around to sustain it. I think a group of local firefighters owned it at one point, as well.

47

A CULTURE DISAPPEARS

Vacant Lots—Photo Credit: Lawrence Miller

The demise of the Rockaway Beach bungalow culture came about for a number of reasons over a couple of decades. But there was a final straw that broke the camel's back. During the early 1980s, Atlantic City was experiencing a renaissance and people believed Rockaway would benefit from a similar revitalization. A coalition petitioned the city to bring legalized gambling to the Rockaways.

Developers began buying up large swaths of property. Many of these transactions were perfectly legal and above board. Many others were not. I heard all sorts of stories of large amounts of cash paid under the table, and when that didn't work, some developers resorted to strong-arm tactics. The owners of the court in which we were living were approached a number of times with offers to buy the property. With each offer and subsequent rejection, the deal got sweeter, but they were not the least bit interested in selling. Soon after they rejected the last offer, a trash can was thrown through the picture window in their living room in the middle of the night. They received all sorts of threats throughout that summer and into the fall.

In the course of one year, huge tracts of land containing hundreds and hundreds of bungalows changed hands, and the summer residents were told to remove their personal belongings and not to return the following summer. Hundreds of bungalows sat empty and boarded up, waiting to be torn down. At the same time, casino developers launched a public relations campaign that would make any Hollywood celebrity green with envy. There were billboards and posters and television commercials, flyers and mailings and pollsters. The powers that be weren't particularly concerned with the summer residents, as most of them rented and could easily be disposed of. No, they targeted the impoverished and lower classes. Those residents were promised high-paying jobs within the grand casinos that were to be built. This would change their lives for the better, they were told. Developers and politicians tried to sway the blue-collar residents, but most of them were the upstanding families of cops and firefighters. They understood what casinos would do to their town and they weren't falling for it.

For better or worse, nothing ever came of it. New York chose not to legalize casino gambling and that was the end of that. Regrettably, however, the worst of the damage had been done and the Rockaway Beach bungalow culture effectively ceased to exist. Rockaway came to resemble a ghost town and, in due course, the abandoned bungalows and deserted courts were razed, and vacant, trash-strewn lots took their place.

Driving around the peninsula, you can still spot a few bungalows here and there. You'll see one standing by itself amidst a sea of vacant lots, or you might come across one surrounded on all sides by shiny, new, townhouse developments. In the last few years, a spate of residential subdivisions has been constructed on the peninsula. It no longer resembles the place where I spent so much of my childhood, and even with the miracle of memory, I still have trouble envisioning it as the vibrant summer community it once was.

48

BEACH PARTIES

Julie, Paul, and the famous watermelon

I threw my first official beach party during the summer of 1982. What would life at the beach be without beach parties? God knows, we certainly had our share of them over the decades. Going through my parents' photo albums, one would think that life in Rockaway was one big beach party after another. Almost every picture shows groups of people on the beach having what seems to be the time of their lives. The men flaunted their physiques for the camera, while the women demonstrated their best bathing beauty poses. Everybody was young, happy, healthy, and carefree. The smiles tell the story. We were all so blissfully unaware of the sun's damaging rays. Photographs such as these can no longer be taken. We've learned too much and, in the process, as one unknown writer once wisely said, our "ignorant innocence has become knowledgeable guilt." Now you know why they're called "the good old days."

Beach parties were a tradition, and each generation was expected to make its mark on this custom. By this time, I had a real job with a big company in the city and my summer was cut back to weekends and holidays. I truly didn't mind this so much because I stayed in the city by myself and thoroughly enjoyed all the freedoms that independence brought. I was young and pretty and popular and making more money than I knew what to do with. I made a ton of new friends at my job and decided it was time to introduce them to a little of the famous Farish hospitality.

It was necessary to have my parents approve the party idea. Even though I would do all the work and undertake the expense, I still required use of the bungalow. I needed a place to store and prepare the food and drinks and some people would need a place to change or shower. I got their approval, proceeded to set a date and sent out invitations.

I worked hard on that party. I wanted it to be great. I wanted people to talk about it for weeks afterward. I had such high hopes. I invited everybody I knew, and just to make sure it was a big crowd, I told Christine to invite her friends, too. I needed to come up with something that would be special, something that nobody had ever seen before. I can't remember where the idea came from, but it was exactly what I was looking for. Any respectable beach party has to have watermelon. Mine did. Only these were special watermelons: They were spiked with vodka. I sat up half the night before the party in the bungalow soaking two giant watermelons with two fifths of vodka.

The big day had finally arrived and I was all set to go. I must have found favor with all the key pagan gods because they provided a stunning summer day. My family helped me cart all the gear down to the beach and a few of my best friends arrived early to help with last-minute preparations. About forty people showed up and it was a good mix: People from work, beach people, family, and family friends. The day was gorgeous, the food delicious, the water warm, the beer cold, the music loud, the crowd young, tan, and having a rousing good time. It was perfect. I should have known something would go wrong.

Oh, there were signs. There are always signs. Obviously, I wasn't paying attention. The first thing I should have noticed was that my father stayed at the party a lot longer than I would have expected. Generally, my parents would put in an appearance to make sure there were no unsavory characters present, said hello to the people they knew, and introduced themselves to those they didn't. They'd stick around for a beer and then be on their way. Mom had left, but Dad was still there. He was standing at the food table eating a piece of watermelon and I walked up to him and mentioned that everything seemed to be going well. He looked at me and said, "Jac, this is the best watermelon I've ever had, it's so sweet, where did you get it?" I told him I picked it up at Bohak's and to go ahead and eat as much as he wanted. I had two, after all. It wasn't until I walked away that I realized the reason it was so sweet was because of the vodka! I forgot to tell him it was spiked! I explained the situation to Barbara and asked her to keep an eye on him. As it turned out, she couldn't watch Dad because she had her hands full with her husband, Paul.

Then, I noticed that everybody was really going for the watermelon. I mean, everybody was eating it and there wasn't much left. I hadn't thought it necessary to mention to anyone that it was soaked in vodka, and I was happy to see that everyone was enjoying it so thoroughly. At twenty, you don't think about the negative effects of alcohol. Getting drunk is supposed to be fun. Hah! I'd had a couple of pieces myself by that point and was feeling no pain. Apparently, Paul wasn't feeling any pain either. Barbara was giving him a hard time about how much he was drinking and she was keeping an eagle eye on him. I tried to get all of us assembled for a group picture and found it nearly impossible. Everyone was staggering around laughing and not paying me one bit of attention. It didn't help matters that Christine was on a roll. I remember standing there with the camera in my hand and thinking, "What is wrong here? It can't be this hard to get a group picture."

Not surprisingly, all hell broke loose. Suddenly, I heard a series of shrill whistles and I turned around to see lifeguards running into the water and I thought to myself, "Oh, some parent wasn't paying attention and now his kid is drowning." Just then, Barbara grabbed me and ran down to the water. Paul was the one drowning! Dad was in trouble, too! All of us ran down to the water's edge screaming and a few of the guys in our group raced in to help. They ended up getting battered by the waves and needed to be rescued, as well. Barbara was hysterical, even after they dragged Paul out of the water. He was tanked! My father was tanked! Everyone was tanked! The lifeguards gave us a scathing lecture about drinking and swimming. Oh God, I wanted to dig a hole and crawl into it. There was no way in hell I was about to tell anyone about the watermelon at that point, and I made Barbara swear to never mention it. Oh, yeah, people talked about that party for years. But what they said was not exactly what I'd had in mind.

49

YOU SAY, "TOMATO"

Dad

The summer of 1983 found my family renting a bungalow in Frumpkin's Court on 99th Street. Frumpkin's was very similar to Hollyhurst, with eight bungalows, four on each side, with alleys in between for the outdoor showers. My sisters and I were adults by this time, so the alley was free of the detritus that accumulates with children present. We had quite a cast of characters in this court, too, another great group of families. Mr. and Mrs. McNulty lived on our left, and the Sullivans lived on our right. My parents still wouldn't install a phone, damn them! But the McNultys had one, and Christine and I relied heavily on it for our various romances.

That summer, my father got it in his head to plant tomatoes. The side alley was empty except for the clothesline. It had plenty of good soil to work with and received direct sun all day long, which is perfect for tomato plants. So he spent the first week of that summer reading up on tomatoes—he'd never grown anything in his life—and preparing the soil. Finally, the day came when he bought the tomato plants and brought them home. He put them in the ground and followed the instructions to the letter. There was no way Gene Sullivan could pass up such a golden opportunity for a gag, and he brought my mother and Mr. McNulty in on his plans.

Every day Dad would check on his plants, watering them and coddling them like a proud parent, and they grew well under his care. Several days after planting them, he went out to check on them early one morning. He promptly ran back into the bungalow and woke up Mom, saying, "Sis, Sis, quick, get up! You're not gonna believe this!" My mother was still half asleep when she followed him outside. "Look at how quick the tomatoes grew!" My mother came promptly awake. My father, not knowing that tomatoes started out green, was looking at the tiny cherry tomatoes that Mom, Gene Sullivan, and Mr. McNulty had painstakingly tied onto his plants the night before!

Dad was thrilled with these results and yelled for Gene to come over and look. He failed to notice that my mother was about to bust her gut trying not to laugh. Before you knew it, half the court was coming over to see these amazing tomato plants. Gene just couldn't help himself, and finally let the cat out of the bag. Boy, was my father pissed! It really was a great joke and all in good fun. Everybody thought so, except Dad. He gave my mother the silent treatment for days, and I swear he didn't give Gene Sullivan the time of day for the rest of that summer. Well, maybe it was just a couple of days.

50

THE IRISH CIRCLE

Patty McCullough, Jackie, Sis, Paul & Barbara

During the summer of 1992, I was in Rockaway for a couple of weeks. My mother, Barbara, and Paul were renting a house in Breezy Point for the summer and both Christine and her husband, and my husband and I, had arranged to be there for a couple of weeks each. I no longer live in the New York area, and I generally visit Mom each year during the week of her birthday. That summer was no different. Her birthday is at the end of July, which just so happens to be the best time to be at the

215

beach in Rockaway. The water temperature is generally in the high-seventies and the jellyfish are not yet out in full force.

We took Mom to dinner at Kennedy's in Breezy Point for her birthday and afterwards drove back to Rockaway to have a few drinks at The Irish Circle. Our friends knew we were in town and agreed to meet up with us after dinner to help my mother celebrate. It turned into quite a crowd. I asked a handful of my friends to join us, and my nephews and a group of their friends also showed up. And Christine, well, she knew just about everyone in town and was downright generous with her invitations. Rob brought a new girlfriend with him. Her name was Monique and she was quite beautiful, however, her great beauty was not the first thing you noticed about her, hence her nickname, "Party Body." The bartender that night, Jerry, was an old beau of Christine's, and most of the other patrons were locals, with whom we had at least a passing acquaintance. Side note: when Chrissy broke up with Jerry years earlier, he started the Rockaway chapter of Woman Haters Anonymous. Last I heard, he's still in love with her.

Unbeknownst to any of us, it was "karaoke night" at the Circle. I had never before experienced this particular phenomenon and thought we should take our somewhat substantial group elsewhere, but I was in the minority. So we commandeered a cluster of tables and ordered drinks. It took only twenty minutes and one Al Green tune to get us started and even I couldn't have imagined what happened next.

A television set above the bar played the video of the song that was being sung on the karaoke machine. When the bartender flipped it on, some guy was on stage singing "Let's Stay Together" by Al Green and the words to the song scrolled along the bottom of the screen. Suddenly, Christine screams, "Oh my God. That's my video!" As fate would have it, she was the principal actress in that particular video which was made a number of years ago. I should add that she wasn't too pleased with it because the camera added pounds that were never there.

Within a matter of moments, everybody in the bar had recognized her and in no time she was up on stage, recreating the video as best she could, much to the annoyance of the guy singing. After that, well, I wouldn't exactly call it a free-for-all but we did take control of the stage and proceeded to sing every song ever written. Yes, we did. We were on a roll and would not be stopped. One by one, both individually and in groups small and large, we took to that stage and sang our collective hearts out. Instead of "Sixteen Candles," a group of us sang "Sixty-Eight Candles" for my mother, even though she kept insisting she was only sixty-seven. I crooned a fairly seductive version of "Hey Big Spender" and at one point there were twenty-seven of us on stage singing "Play That Funky Music White Boy" at the top of our lungs. It had to be the most successful karaoke night ever in the history of the Rockaways. Unquestionably, we were completely tanked, but we ended up having the time of our lives.

I returned to Rockaway for my mother's eightieth birthday in July 2005. Mom spent the entire summer at the beach every year and had no desire to go into the city unless it was absolutely necessary. Several months earlier, my sisters and I, during our weekly conference call, had discussed the upcoming celebration with Mom.

She nixed plans for an elaborate party at a fabulous restaurant in Manhattan, so we were left with the extremely slim restaurant choices at the beach. After much discussion and numerous phone calls to various restaurants, we decided to celebrate her birthday at The Irish Circle, the scene of numerous and varied debaucheries over the years.

My first thought was no, no, no! Not the same old bar in the same old neighborhood with the same old faces! We need to do something different, something new, something fabulous! Since Barbara was the only sibling living in New York at that time, she was the point person for this operation. And since she did all the legwork, she had the last word. Hence, The Irish Circle.

We limited the invitations to family members living in the NYC area. Otherwise, the guest list would have gotten completely out of hand, and since I was paying for this shindig, I had several good reasons to keep it manageable, fiscally and otherwise. First off, there were no hotels or motels in Rockaway Beach. Well, that's not exactly true. Rooms were available but no place where I'd stay, much less recommend to a family member. My mom's place at the beach was tiny, and although she had a pull-out sofa and an extra cot, Christine and I would be bunking with her and, it goes without saying, straining her last nerve. There was absolutely no place to put out-of-town guests. So, not only were invitations restricted to NYC area family members, they were limited to family members with wheels due to the woeful lack of decent public transportation.

Secondly, and it took weeks of negotiations on this one, we couldn't invite any of our friends. Between Barbara, Christine, and myself, we would have had half the population of several boroughs in attendance, and as I've already mentioned, I was financing this operation. This was a particularly tough decision because, in our family, we all knew each other's friends and our friends knew and loved our parents. I had to be tough on this point even though Barbara called and pleaded with me every other day. Eventually, I told her that if she wanted to invite any of her friends, she'd have to pay for them. That was the end of that discussion.

Not only was it a great party, it was an appropriate party because there's nothing in the world like coming home. Not just for me, but for everyone who attended. My Uncle Tony Farish, patriarch of the Farish clan since he was the last surviving brother; my cousins, Fran and Lorraine and their families; my Uncle Mickey McCloskey and Aunt Isabelle; my godfather, Pat Vitale; my nephews, Robert and Harry and their wives; and Mom, my sisters, and our spouses. Each one of us had a history in Rockaway, some peoples' are longer than others', some peoples' are more nefarious. Despite my initial doubts, everyone was more than comfortable at The Irish Circle because it has been our place for as long as we can remember. Rockaway is our home-away-from-home, and no matter how long we stay away, it always feels good to be back.

Sometime during the early 2000s, Barbara called to inform me that The Irish Circle had closed down and was boarded up. I was stunned by this news and asked why. She didn't know but guessed that maybe the state shut it down because of the illegal gambling that was known to go on there. She sounded terribly depressed. Of course, we all made bets there over the years and I had a hard time believing that it was closed down for good. I mean, it had been there forever. So I called Rob and asked him about it. He told me, "No. They're just doing some remodeling and installing OTB windows in the bar. It'll be open again soon." Thank God! I guess that's one way to get rid of illegal bookmaking—replace it with a state-sanctioned version.

Over the years, we all experienced some of life's significant moments within the confines of The Irish Circle. There were wakes, weddings, bar room brawls, softball victories, birthdays, anniversaries, and first dates.

Sometime during the late '90s, while visiting Mom, I ran into a guy on whom I'd had a whopping crush years earlier. Rob and some other friends and I went to The Irish Circle on a Saturday night to hear a band. The place was packed and it was five deep at the bar, but we'd arrived fairly early and I commandeered a barstool and stayed put. Walking in that crowd would be murder on your toes. Anyway, Rob was off chasing the pretty girls and I was sitting there nursing a beer and bemoaning the fact that there weren't any good-looking men to gawk at. By midnight, I was tired, bored, and ready to go home when I spotted him across the bar. Just then, Rob came by to check on me and noticed that someone had piqued my interest. I pointed out the individual to him and he said, "Oh, that's Timmy." I looked at him with wide eyes and said, "You don't mean Timmy. Is that Timmy?" He replied, "Yeah, he's on the job." In other words, he's a firefighter! Could this get any better? I almost fell off my barstool. Rob laughed and disappeared into the crowd.

Timmy. Wow. He had lived up the street from us on 101st Street during the summer and was a Bronx boy the rest of the year. All of the girls had a crush on Timmy—he was so damn cute! He's what is referred to as "black Irish"—with an olive complexion, dark hair, dark eyes. He was tall and lanky and possessed a shy smile. Oh yeah, all the girls would get dreamy-eyed when he came round. He ran with an older crowd that never really crossed paths with mine. I hadn't seen him in a number of years and had pretty much forgotten about him. Trust me, he grew up real good.

So, back to the bar that night: I fixed my gaze on him, willing him to look at me. Eventually our eyes locked on each other and I slowly crooked my finger at him and gestured to come over. He pointed his finger at his chest and mouthed, "Me?" and I smiled and nodded, and he started to make his way around the bar. What was I doing? I had no idea what to say to him! He would never remember me!

I turned around on my barstool and there he was. I smiled at him and said, "Do you remember me?" and he said, "Of course I remember you, Jackie. How you doin'?" and then he gave me a great big hug and kiss. I was so happy he remembered me! We talked for quite a while and caught up on each other's lives and families. It was during that conversation I discovered he was only a year older than I was. If I had run with the older crowd in Rockaway, I might have dated him years ago. Yet another missed opportunity of my youth and one I truly regret. Oh, but what a night! You couldn't wipe the smile off my face for a week.

51

CLUB 101

Chris Frazier, Sis, Jackie, Jeanie Callahan

In 1984, I moved to California, following a career path. I was the last child to leave my parents' home, and the first to move out of the New York area. I believe it's the distance from my family and our history that allows me to recall my childhood so clearly. But every year, I flew back to New York and spent a couple of weeks at the beach with Mom, usually for her birthday in July.

The Callahan's bungalows were the last holdouts on 101st Street. When I was in town for Mom's birthday in July 2006, we were invited to a barbeque at Callahan's Court, which was then called Club 101. Bill Callahan had bought two neighboring courts and had been renting the bungalows to friends and family members. That summer, they held a barbeque every Saturday night because it was to be the "Last Summer of the Bungalows." The plan was to tear them down over the winter and build condos, which had already been purchased by family members and select friends.

It was great to see all those people from my childhood, from the days when the bungalows ruled. Some of them I hadn't seen in twenty or twenty-five years. I immediately recognized Jeannie; she hadn't changed a bit. It took me a minute to place Stacy, who lost her baby flab and turned into a beautiful young woman. Never in a million years would I have recognized Chris! He was no longer the skinny, tow-headed kid with hair hanging in his eyes! I met several new husbands, wives, and children; well, they're new to me, anyway. As I've said, things change. I was sorry to hear the last of the bungalows would be demolished, but thrilled to know the Callahans and Fraziers were planning to stay. Mrs. Callahan took Mom, Christine, and I for a last look through their bungalow and showed us the construction plans for the new condominiums.

The following summer, Mom and I took a stroll down 101st Street and sure enough, Callahan's Court was gone. A year after that, I saw a "for sale" sign on the fence surrounding the vacant lot. The Callahans had given up on Rockway, too.

52

BEACH BAPTISMS

Jessie and Godmother Jackie

When my sister Christine married her first husband, Gary, she moved to his hometown of Pittsburgh, Pennsylvania. During their first year of marriage, she became pregnant with her first child, Jesse. He was born in May 1993, and my family already had plans to rent a home in Breezy Point that summer. My mother would stay at the beach and Barbara and Paul would join her most weekends. My husband John and I planned to visit for ten days in July, so Christine decided to have Jesse christened at St. Thomas More Catholic Church in Breezy Point while we were in town, since we were to be the godparents.

We planned a party for the occasion and everyone we knew was invited—aunts, uncles, cousins, family friends, work friends, city friends, beach friends, a few old boyfriends, some random acquaintances, and even a couple of frenemies. As the new mother, Christine would be the center of attention, and she really shined, which is just what she had planned to do. The party was a great success.

In 2000, Christine became pregnant with her second child, Austin, who was born in October. That year, John and I planned to be in New York for the holidays, so Christine decided to have Austin christened in Breezy Point while we were in town. She liked the idea of both of her children being christened at the same church. It was the dead of winter, and we weren't renting a house at the beach, so we planned to have the christening party at a restaurant in Rockaway Beach that was large enough to accommodate the many guests. The church was reserved, the invitations sent, and the menu finalized.

Christine and her family, now living in Florida, stayed at Mom's apartment in the city, while John and I stayed at The Waldorf-Astoria Hotel. The morning of the baptism, we awoke to a massive blizzard, now referred to as the December 2000 nor'easter.

The holidays are always a busy time. Between shopping and wrapping gifts, attending parties, getting together with friends, and taking part in all the fun New York City holiday traditions—like going to see the Radio City Christmas Spectacular, visiting the Rockefeller Center Christmas tree, ogling the department stores' window décor, sitting on Santa's lap at Macy's—none of us paid any attention to the weather reports. We didn't have time to sit around watching the news! But we did that morning.

New York Governor George Pataki declared a state of emergency and asked everyone to stay home. All businesses would be closed and only first responders would be on the roads. All mass transit was shut down.

After staring out the hotel window at the white-out conditions, I started making phone calls. I called Christine first and told her we had to cancel everything. She brushed off my concerns. I tried to explain how bad the situation was, but she wasn't having it. I told her we wouldn't drive out to Breezy but she was adamant. "I came here to baptize my son and I'm going to baptize my son."

Mom then got on the phone. "I already told her none of us should be on the road, but Christine is going to do what Christine wants to do. She isn't listening to me." Then Charlie, Christine's second husband, got on the phone. He was pleading with her to call the whole thing off, telling her being on the road would put the kids in danger. Then I called Barbara and Paul and explained that Christine was going through with it even though none of us would attend. Barbara was infuriated, screaming that Christine was out of her mind. In the meantime, the restaurant called to tell us they would not be opening and cancelled the reservation.

Christine called the church and the priest agreed to do the baptism. Christine told Charlie that if he didn't go, she would drive herself and the two kids. Charlie didn't have a choice, so he drove Christine, eight-year-old Jesse, and two-month-old Austin, all the way out to Breezy Point. The only other person to attend was Austin's godmother, Jackie Pareja, who, unbelievably, drove in from New Jersey.

Christine always had a hard time with the word "no."

53

SEPTEMBER 11, 2001

L.A. Times newspaper article

The populace of the Rockaways, as you know by now, was overwhelmingly of Irish descent. It's a close-knit community with extremely large families and just about everyone has a member working for the New York Police Department or the New York Fire Department, or both. Many of these families have generations of service within these departments, and every kid with whom I grew up took their entry exams. I took the police exam for the first time when I was fifteen, and again at seventeen. At that time in New York City, there was a four-year waiting list to serve. I scored a 97 on my first written test and it still took four years before I was called for the physical and medical exams. So, Rockaway kids take the tests and then go about their lives, waiting for the call. They go to school and then to work, usually getting a job through someone they know on Wall Street, or in the insurance industry, or maybe in real estate. But those jobs are placeholders as they wait for the call for their real careers to begin.

I spoke to Robert, a lifelong Rockaway resident two days after the September Eleventh terrorist attacks. He'd been with the NYFD until his retirement several years ago. In the aftermath of the devastation, after finding out my family members were all safe and accounted for, I called to check on him. It turns out he wasn't on duty that awful Tuesday morning. He was surfing in Far Rockaway and saw the mushroom cloud from the water. He reported in immediately and was sent to cover a firehouse in Chinatown, all of whose members were at "ground zero." That was the first time I'd heard that phrase.

I spoke to Robert on Thursday and was so relieved to hear that he was okay that I wasn't ready for what came next. He told me that Rockaway had been decimated by the attack and started reciting the names of the dead and missing. With each name, my heart skipped a beat. These were my childhood friends, kids I grew up with, people I knew for decades. It was unfathomable. He kept saying things like, "You remember John, he's a Captain now." "Remember Walter? He always hung out up on the boardwalk?" "Remember Richie from Allen's Deli? His son Richie was just three weeks out of the academy."

I asked Robert about other people we knew, like Timmy (firefighter) and Tommy (transit police), both Rockaway summer residents. They were okay. The local paper, *The Wave,* reported that as many as 100 people from the Rockaways and Breezy Point were still missing at the time I spoke to Rob. My brother-in-law, Paul Devereaux, is a Breezy boy, born and bred. I spoke with him a few days later and he recited the names of his childhood friends and neighbors who were unaccounted for. He was heartbroken, as we all were.

I read the list of dead and missing uniformed service personnel the *Los Angeles Times* ran. I recognized too many names. Running my finger down the list, I came across one name and my heart dropped. William, Staten Island, Rescue 4, Queens. Remember my boyfriend Billy with the loud Cadillac? He was from Staten Island, and yes, he too, became a firefighter. I don't know if these Williams are one and the same. I don't want to know and have never asked.

Many towns in and around New York boast residents who work as first responders and they were all hit hard by that tragedy. God bless them all. This place—Rockaway—this is my place, and these are the people I knew.

54

ROCKAWAY, FOREVER

Sunset over Jamaica Bay

I reside in Southern California these days, home of the Beach Boys, land of Gidget, domain of Malibu Barbie. I actually live at the beach, which shouldn't come as too much of a surprise, since I consider myself an island girl and beach baby, albeit the island is Manhattan and the beach is Rockaway. Unfortunately, I don't spend much time on the sand, and I've swum in the cold, gray, Pacific waters all of half a dozen times in forty years. This is a sorry state of affairs when you take into account Southern California's renowned history of frolicking in the surf, sun, and sand.

It's not the beach of my childhood. The sand isn't as fine, the water isn't as warm, and I find that deep ocean trench just off the coast somewhat unsettling. For years, I've taken a daily run along the shoreline and have yet to spot a starfish, a jellyfish, or a horseshoe crab. I see a pod of porpoises almost daily and I've spotted whales during the migration season, but these creatures are foreign to me and, since there's no opportunity for any kind of interaction—you stand on the shore and watch them from afar—I've yet to achieve a comfort level with their presence. I'm intimidated by the Pacific.

Up until 2012, I had returned to Rockaway every summer and was always surprised at how many of the people I grew up with had managed to keep roots in that place. Even with all the changes, it was comforting to know I could always return and still feel at home. When I would visit, we'd fall back on the same old traditions and habits of years gone by and I found myself at a loss to explain what a comfort that was to me. And I swam. Oh boy, did I swim. I spent the days in the ocean and instead of sitting up on the sand in a beach chair, I found myself sitting in the shallows letting the water lap over me. I knew my time there was limited and didn't want to waste a moment of it.

I could take a walk on the boardwalk or go down to the beach and still run into some of the same families and friends from my childhood, and more often than not, I'd get to meet a whole new generation of offspring. I would meet my friend Barbara for a drink or two. I'd take a walk with Mom and go to The Irish Circle for dinner. I'd stop to buy a sandwich at Allen's Deli, even though Richie Allen doesn't own it anymore. Many of these people would fail to recognize me without some prompting on my part, but I remembered them all, despite the changes the passing years have made.

One glorious summer day I found myself sitting on the beach with a circle of friends from the past and present. My sister, Christine, was there along with her then five-year-old son, Jesse. Robert and his latest girlfriend were present, along with Julie Gold, a friend of mine from the city who was a frequent visitor to our bungalow over the years. A guy friend of Christine's came out from the city for the day and our friend, Barbara, who was taking a stroll along the boardwalk, spotted us and joined our little group. It was late in the afternoon, about five o'clock, and the beach was deserted. We sat with our chairs in a circle, completely relaxed, sipping cold beer, catching up on each other's lives, and reminiscing about the past, while Jesse sat in the center creating sandcastles with his pail and shovel.

At some point, I was viewing this scene from a distance. I saw my parents and their friends sitting in this same spot, only I was the child building the sandcastles. And then I saw my sister, Barbara, and her friends with their children playing at their feet. I sincerely hoped Jesse and my other nieces and nephews would find themselves in this same place, someday, with their children playing in the sand, just like the generations before them. Just like we were.

But it wasn't to be . . .

55

SUPERSTORM SANDY

Superstorm Sandy destruction, Breezy Point—
Photo Credit: Cassie Mullholand

I believed my family would always have a presence in Rockaway. It was such an essential component of our family story, and I couldn't imagine not having ties to the place that played such a vital role in shaping who we've become. I've lived in California for four decades, yet every summer, I returned to Rockaway for a few weeks.

Superstorm Sandy changed all that. Overnight, the history of our seaside idyll was literally washed away . . . .

It wasn't unusual for Mom to stay at her place in Rockaway well into the fall, so long as the weather held. My sisters and I took to calling her "Yo Yo Ma" because she bounced back and forth from the city to the beach so frequently.

In late October 2012, the news outlets began reporting on Hurricane Sandy, and as with every major storm, we were glued to the newscasts to see what track it would take. When it looked like the path was headed toward the northeast, we called Mom and told her to get back to the city immediately. She insisted we were overreacting, and it was a struggle to convince her to leave. She did, eventually, thank God.

We all watched the coverage of Sandy slamming into the eastern seaboard with unimaginable fury, and Rockaway bore the full impact of it. The combination of location and sea level altitude doomed the Rockaway peninsula.

Since there's a phone in everyone's pocket, there was plenty of raw footage—most of which had to be seen to be believed. The waves were tall enough to crash over two-story structures three blocks from the beach. With the bay water rising on one side and the ocean hammering the other, the entire peninsula was well underwater.

Most people played it safe and evacuated, but there were those— there are always *those*—who chose to stay and ride it out. Some of them ended up abandoning their swamped homes, struggling through chest-high water and hurricane strength wind gusts.

As if the torrential rain, gale force winds, and ocean rage weren't life threatening enough, a fire started by electrical wiring raged through Breezy Point, destroying well over 100 homes. My brother-in-law Paul's childhood home was one of them. Too many more homes were destroyed, by both fire and flood, throughout the Rockaways and other coastal communities.

Once the storm had passed, the extent of the damage was beyond comprehension. The boardwalk was gone. Chunks of concrete pilings offered the only proof it ever existed. Whole blocks were leveled Homes were torn from their foundations, others collapsed into piles of rubble. Businesses and restaurants that had served the community for decades were torn apart or completely destroyed. Photographs of the damage are all over the internet, and looking at them all these years later, it's still difficult to grasp just how severe Superstorm Sandy was.

The lobby and first floor of my mother's building were inundated with flood waters, but her apartment was on the second floor, and luckily, sustained no real damage. Several weeks later she returned to survey the devastation. By that time, city crews had created a massive sand dune where the boardwalk once was, to keep shorefront homes and businesses safe from further high tides.

Mom took photos, sent them to us, and described the devastation during several phone conversations. She stayed in Rockaway only one night since none of the stores or supermarkets were open. She closed up the apartment for the winter and returned to the city.

I intended to stay with her the following summer for a couple of weeks, but she told me not to come. There was still a massive, debris-filled sand dune and no beach. And she had decided to put her place up for sale. The destruction was just too much, and she believed it would be a very, very long time before Rockaway could, or would, rise from the ashes.

My sisters and I were devastated by this news. It was impossible to imagine that, after sixty years, we wouldn't have a home in the Rockaways.

Photo Credit: Howard Schwach

Photo Credit: Howard Schwach

Photo Credit: Joanie Hess

Photo Credit: Peter Brady

Photo Credit: Joanie Hess

Photo Credit: Cassie Mullholland

Photo Credit: Joanie Hess

56

THE END OF AN ERA

Sunset over Marine Parkway bridge

While Superstorm Sandy severed all connections to Rockaway for my family, I still return to New York a few times each year to see friends and family and attend celebratory events.

My husband and I were in town a few years ago and on the day we were leaving, had to travel from New Jersey to JFK. The route would take us via Staten Island and the Verrazano Bridge, and we could make a detour through Rockaway. I hadn't been there in over a decade and wanted to see what had become of my childhood summer stomping ground.

We drove over the Verrazano Bridge into Brooklyn, took the Belt Parkway to the Marine Parkway Bridge, and headed east on Beach

Channel Drive. None of my family members had returned to Rockaway since Mom sold her place, and I had no idea what to expect.

As we drove through Neponsit and Belle Harbor, I saw that many of the stately, old, clapboard homes had survived, alongside new construction. 116th Street is still a commercial zone comprised of small businesses, with some new multi-story housing. Tribute Park, located at the end of the street on the beach with views of the city, is a new addition. It pays homage to those who lost their lives on 9/11. The old brick subway station and firehouse still look exactly the same. It was reassuring to see the street bustling with people shopping and going about their business.

Heading east on Rockaway Beach Boulevard, we spotted several new multi-unit housing developments that were once vacant lots, across the street from the Dayton Towers. As we approached 102nd Street, I felt some apprehension.

There was some new construction between the El and the boulevard, and as we turned the corner, my heart leapt at the sight of The Irish Circle! Sitting on the same corner since 1893, it boasted new siding, a new sign, and the tower was still in place. (Since this was written, I discovered The Irish Circle has been demolished. What a shame.)

We drove up 102nd Street to Shorefront Parkway for our first look at the boardwalk. The boards have been replaced with concrete. It looks to be the same width, with railings on both sides and benches facing the ocean. An attempt has been made to restore dune grasses. There were never dune grasses during the decades my family spent in Rockaway, and it's a smart improvement.

We drove up and down the streets where my family lived and around the wider neighborhood. We saw several townhouse developments on Rockaway Beach Boulevard and a couple along Shorefront Parkway, right across the street from the beach. A few of the large, old, beach cottages on 94th Street and 95th Street have been renovated with care and look like they might have looked 150 years ago. The newer apartment/condo complexes built on those blocks seem awfully incongruent.

There were a few surprises along the way, too. Rockaway Taco, a stand squished between two buildings, boasted a line half-way down the block. The Rockaway Beach Surf Club on 87th Street is a bar and event space serving the surf-minded community. The Bungalow Bar sits at the foot of Cross Bay Bridge. It boasts views of Jamaica Bay, making lunch on the deck a must. The boutique Rockaway Hotel opened on 108th Street. Finally, a real hotel in Rockaway! I would never have guessed it, but Rockaway has become hip! And yes, there are still a few bungalows tucked away, here and there.

Thomas Wolfe wrote, "You can't go home again." According to Wikipedia, "The saying is meant to infer how nostalgia causes us to view the past in an overly positive light, and how humans tend to remember people and places from our upbringing in static terms." I don't agree with that sentiment. To return home after so many years would be different, of course. But it might be better. Who knows?

When one lives near, in, or on the water—no matter how far you may roam—the sea inevitably draws you back. Not unlike marine life, most people will gravitate to that with which they're familiar, whether it's actual experience or something in the genetic material. Salmon return to the streams and rivers they were born in, to spawn; the magnetic compass of sea turtles conveys them to the beaches of their birth to lay their eggs; whales will travel 3,000 miles to their birthplace to deliver their calves.

It wouldn't surprise me if some day, a family member of a future generation returns to the Rockaways and puts down roots. And when they do, if I'm still around, I'll be there.

The End

ACKNOWLEDGMENTS

Imagine writing a memoir about a setting that no longer exists, and people you haven't seen or spoken to in 50+ years. Not easy. But, much easier because of the internet! I'd really like to thank those I contacted, completely out of the blue, for returning my calls and messages. For those I was unable to contact, know that I wanted to include photos of you, but due to the litigious environment we live in, I couldn't take that chance.

A big thank you to the generous individuals on various social media sites that gave me permission to use their images. It's comforting to know there are so many others out there with fond memories of their time in Rockaway.

This book would never have gotten to the finish line if not for the A team at KP Publishing! Never having written a book before, I'm indebted to Editor Laurel Davis, who gently provided direction and insight. Illustrator Juan Roberts, captured beautifully the fragmentary nature of my book with his cover art. How did he know I had Post-its stuck all over my desk as I wrote? Publisher Willa Robinson reassured me that I had a story to tell. It was a privilege and joy to work with her.

Writing a book and finding a publisher you're comfortable working with, are just two parts of the equation. Having an ace team to put it out into the world is another. I'm grateful for my PR team on both coasts:

Local superwoman, Tonya McKenzie, Founder, Sands and Shores, and publicist extraordinaire, and mia cugina, Jacqueline Giaccio.

To our bungalow neighbors and friends, you clearly made a lasting impression on my family and I, for us to remember you all so fondly and vividly. The "good old days" is a real thing, and we were there!

To my remarkable extended family, my childhood would not have been the same without your steady presence. How fortunate am I to have grown up among such a loving, gregarious clan?!?

To Mom, Dad, Barbara and Christine, it's been an extraordinary, fun-filled ride. Without you, there would be no stories.

Lastly, I couldn't have completed this undertaking without the support of my husband, JB. It was his suggestion that my stories could be turned into a book. JB has always encouraged my many, completely random, endeavors. And there have been A LOT. I keep things interesting, and he keeps me laughing. Spouses, partners, cohorts, mates, companions, duo, team, comrades, allies, collaborators, buddies. . . . We are a gang of two!

ABOUT THE AUTHOR

Jackie Balestra has been writing professionally since 2008 and has had articles published in local, regional, and national publications. After writing for Examiner.com for several years, in 2011 she created a website, southbaybyjackie.com, that provided a calendar of events for the South Bay area of Los Angeles, boasting more than a million users.

Jackie also co-hosted a popular podcast for ten years, called "The South Bay Show," on Blog Talk Radio. She retired her website and podcast in 2021 when she and her husband purchased a motor coach. She is currently blogging about their RV adventures via her Facebook platform, "RamblinJax" (https://www.facebook.com/RamblinJax/).

In her book, *The Rockaway Chronicles*, Jackie recounts several life-altering events her family and the Rockaway Beach community encountered over the decades. From bad urban planning and policies to the wrath of Mother Nature, Rockaway endured difficulties that significantly transformed what was once a vibrant, seasonal, coastal community.

www.ingramcontent.com/pod-product-compliance
Lightning Source LLC
Chambersburg PA
CBHW030411130626
46549CB00004B/1723